GRUENEWALD DRAWINGS

THE DRAWINGS OF
MATHIS GOTHART NITHART

CALLED

EDITED BY

GUIDO SCHOENBERGER

H. BITTNER AND COMPANY · NEW YORK

1948

Printed in the United States of America

UNDER THE AUSPICES OF
THE INSTITUTE OF FINE ARTS
EDGAR W. ANTHONY FUND
NEW YORK UNIVERSITY

CONTENTS

Key to marginal notes of Introduction:

Numbers refer to original drawings
A numbers refer to appendix
S numbers refer to sources

PREFACE

THE purpose of this edition of Gruenewald's drawings is to give a complete account of all the drawings known at the present time. Older publications are no longer complete, besides being mostly out of print and difficult to obtain.

The introduction attempts to convey the importance of these drawings, each of which is a most personal confession of the master's artistic aims. A short account of the painter's life and principal works is followed by a description of Gruenewald's general approach to the problem of drawing, his drawing technique and style, the relation of his drawings to his own paintings, and finally of their effect on the master's contemporary schools as well as their place in the history of art.

The sequence of the catalogue raisonné and the plates aims to establish a definite chronology, as far as that is possible.

The understanding consideration of the publisher, Mr. Herbert Bittner, made it possible to reproduce, in addition to the original drawings, an appendix of plates reproducing the paintings of Gruenewald for which the drawings were preparatory, and works by other masters, iconographically significant in relation to Gruenewald's work. Paintings mentioned in the introduction or in the catalogue, not reproduced in the appendix, are referred to by their plate numbers in Arthur Burkhard's book on Matthias Gruenewald, Cambridge 1936, a very good survey and characterization of the master's works, and the only one existing in the English language. The "Sources" constitute a further supplement. This selection of quotations from original documents was determined by their bearing on the drawings themselves, or on salient facts in Gruenewald's life that help to clarify certain problems concerning the drawings. These quotations from the original documents are mostly taken from the book of W. K. Zuelch, Der historische Gruenewald, Munich 1938, which is by far the most comprehensive publication on the master in recent years, containing much valuable information, often hidden in notes and appendices. Besides the book of H. A. Schmid never loses its great documentary value.

For permission to reproduce from new photographs of the originals, I have to thank Mr. Le Roy Backus of Seattle, the National Museum of Stockholm and the Cabinet des Desseins of the Louvre. Except for the facsimile reproductions in original size, the older reproductions in general books on Gruenewald or in smaller publications, are much too strong in their contrast of light and dark, and do not convey the floating unity

7

of the originals. Publisher and printer have bent every effort towards a faithful reproduction of Gruenewald's own work.

I would like to express my gratitude to Professor Walter W. S. Cook of the Institute of Fine Arts of New York University for his interest and kind help in the publication of this book. I would also like to thank Professor Martin Weinberger of the same Institute, Dr. Phyllis Bober of Wellesley College and Professor Erwin Panofsky of the Institute of Advanced Studies of Princeton for many most useful suggestions. Miss Frances Huemer and Mr. W. H. Olp helped me in the reconstruction of the Aschaffenburg Altar. Finally I have to thank Miss Beatrice Hudson for revising the English and reading the proofs.

INTRODUCTION

EARLY IN JANUARY, 1664, A TRAVELLING FRENCHMAN OF DISTINC-
tion, Balthasar de Monconys, spent some time in Frankfurt-on-Main. One day,
guided by Jacob Marrel, a painter of French extraction, and a shrewd art dealer,
he went to visit Abraham Schelkens. Schelkens was a very rich man, member of a
family from Malines which had fled from religious persecution in 1572. He owned one of the
best private collections in Frankfurt; his large town house was open to art lovers who could
there enjoy a collection, evidently brought together with great discrimination and quite different from the usual confusion of a *Kunst- und Wunderkammer*. There were, in addition to
paintings, beautiful volumes with prints by Israel van Meckenem and the engravings and
woodcuts of Duerer, including the Triumphal Arch. So far, de Monconys must surely have
enjoyed the collection, but to his experienced eye it may have contained little of unusual
character. Finally however, he was confronted with a volume of drawings by a master whom   *S 15*
he did not know, because—as he remarks in his diary—the artist was little known in France,
though all his Frankfurt friends told him that in Germany he was more highly esteemed than
Duerer. One must realize that this means a great deal, because during the sixteenth and seventeenth centuries there was hardly any work of high quality in Germany which was not ascribed
to Duerer if by chance the real artist was unknown. De Monconys quotes the name of the master as a certain "Martin d'Aschaffenbourg," but there is no doubt that he meant the painter
Mathis von Aschaffenburg, i.e., Gruenewald.

Eleven years later, in 1675, Joachim von Sandrart, the "German Vasari" relates in the   *S 17, 18*
"Teutsche Academie," his famous collection of artists' biographies, that Schelkens bought
the precious drawings from the widow of the painter Philipp Uffenbach. Around the year 1600
this painter had been the most faithful and at the same time a quite original follower of the
great sixteenth-century German masters. According to Sandrart, Schelkens paid a very high
price for the drawings, because Uffenbach's widow knew how much her late husband had ap-
preciated them. Sandrart himself remembered the great esteem in which Uffenbach held these
drawings: more than fifty years before, when still a schoolboy, he had sometimes stepped into
Uffenbach's workshop, where the old master showed him, as some of his most beloved treas-
ures, drawings by Gruenewald. He had obtained them according to Sandrart from his teacher,
Adam Grimmer, a painter living in Mainz, who in turn must have inherited them from his
father Hans, said to be a pupil of Gruenewald himself. It is important to note that these drawings received from Sandrart no less praise than Gruenewald's great altar-pieces at Frankfurt
and Mainz which he also knew from his own experience.[1]

Sandrart, who is often rather superficial in his praise and rather easy-going in stating facts,
becomes surprisingly serious when he is speaking of Gruenewald. In judging the source value
of his writing, his research on the master is found to have reached very positive and correct

9

conclusions regarding his works, while very uncertain and partly wrong ones regarding his biography. Perhaps Sandrart's very ambition to ascertain new facts about his hero led him into error concerning his real name. Having heard from Uffenbach that in his lifetime the master was called Matthaeus von Aschaffenburg—which in fact was not completely correct either, as the name was Matthias, not Matthaeus—he must have received the information during the publication of his book that the master's family name was Gruenewald. Correcting the manuscript in several places, but not throughout, he introduced this name which has been used almost exclusively ever since.

S 13   Today we know from careful reading and interpretation of the sources[2] that the name of the painter, whose monogram MGN is found on two of his most important works,[3] was in reality Mathis Gothart Nithart. But Sandrart's name "Gruenewald" is so firmly connected with the master of the Isenheim Altar that it is practical to continue to use it as a surname. Once the correct name was known, a biography could be established which is quite different from Sandrart's. Sandrart's "Gruenewald" is a very lonely man living in an unhappy marriage who dies about 1510. Mathis Gothart Nithart was never married. He was court painter to the Arch-

S 6   bishop of Mainz, Uriel von Gemmingen (1508-1514), and to his better known successor Albrecht von Brandenburg (1514-1545) who became Cardinal in 1518. Thus at least as far as his position is concerned, the painter was not at all remote from the active life of his time, on the contrary he was right in the center of the religious and social turmoil. The sources show that the man and the artist was taking part and choosing sides in these struggles.

S 11   Master Mathis was born in Wuerzburg about 1465. He was working as a master already at some time near 1490 in Aschaffenburg, on the Main River, upstream from Frankfurt, a little town, but important as the residence of the Archbishop of Mainz. In 1501 he moved his workshop to a still smaller place, Seligenstadt, between Aschaffenburg and Frankfurt, also within the Archbishopric of Mainz. He kept his workshop in Seligenstadt for more than twenty years, until 1525.

One of the most puzzling facts concerning the master's art is that prior to his settling down in Seligenstadt we do not know of any work, either painting or drawing, which can be ascribed to his hand with certainty. Almost everything published until now as a work of the young Gruenewald has to be discarded, except perhaps the delicately painted portrait of Pfalzgraf Friedrich, now at the Museum of Heidelberg, painted between 1480 and 1490. But even this remains very hypothetical.[4] From the master's established work however, it can be concluded fairly well that he received his most decisive training in the workshop of the Master of the House-book, who most probably lived in Mainz. His excitingly progressive engravings, done in dry point, anticipate, in the field of graphic arts, Gruenewald's painterly style. In the decade between 1490 and 1500 Gruenewald seems to have travelled southwards to Augsburg where he became acquainted with the art of Hans Holbein the Elder. In 1501 Holbein himself appeared in the Middle Rhine country, painting the high altar of the Dominican church in Frankfurt. From him Gruenewald learned the effect of glowing colors on a dark blue, almost black ground which he developed most strikingly later in his crucifixions.

10

When he settled in Seligenstadt in 1501, his fame must have been already firmly established. Soon he was called for important commissions: as early as 1502-1503 to Bindlach near Bamberg (Burkhard pl. 1). In connection with this order, contact was perhaps first established with Duerer's workshop in Nuremberg. Shortly after 1503 another commission came from Aschaffenburg to paint the Derision of Christ. In 1508-1509 Guido Guersi, the Prior of the convent *A 1* of the Antonites at Isenheim in Alsace gave to Master Mathis the greatest order of his life: to *A 7* paint the triple wings of the main altar of this monastery. Guersi was an Italian; it is a proof *A 9-16* of his independence as well as of Gruenewald's fame that he entrusted the gigantic work to a German who was most unItalian in spirit. Yet it is possible that he suggested to the master a trip to Italy before starting the work. Mathis was not in Seligenstadt in the years 1509 and 1510. This may well have been the fateful period of Gruenewald's life in which he was confronted with Venetian color and the modelling of Leonardo.

At the same time that he was working on the Isenheim Altar Gruenewald probably came in contact with Duerer again, in connection with the order of Jacob Heller for another altar: the Assumption of the Virgin in the Dominican church of Frankfurt.[5] Heller, not satisfied with the exterior view of his altar, ordered the addition of stationary wings representing four saints in grisaille, two of which are fortunately preserved (Frankfurt, Staedel Museum, Burkhard pl. 8). Within the painted work of Gruenewald, these grisailles form a most important parallel to the master's drawings. He succeeded in developing in this colorless scheme a maximum of refined and rich tone, ranging from warm yellowish gray and silver-gray to the most variegated shades of mother-of-pearl. The abundance and agitation of the color bring to life forms full of the same strange and powerful spirit which we find also in the drawings of this great period, between 1510 and 1515.

In this period his official position at the court of Mainz is more clearly indicated in the sources: he was the supervisor of the building activities of the Archbishop and as such was concerned, in 1511, with the construction of a large new room in the castle of Aschaffenburg, the most important feature of which was to be a huge chimney-piece. He hired professional workmen for the execution, but he is quoted in the sources, not only as "Master Mathis, the painter," but also as "architect" and even once as "painter and mason." Thus it cannot be doubted that he was the leading artist for the enterprise, and drawings for the chimney-piece, which was surely meant to be richly decorated, must have existed. The work itself disappeared when the castle was completely rebuilt in about 1600. However, the frame of the Altar of the Virgin of the Snows in the Collegiate Church of Aschaffenburg, signed with his mono- *A 24* gram, proves his skill in architectural ornamentation. Furthermore, the painter had also a great reputation as an expert in the field of engineering. In 1517, in the midst of the greatest activity, while he was painting altars for Tauberbischofsheim and for the Cathedral of Mainz, he was called as an expert to pronounce upon the construction of a fountain built by another master in front of the Collegiate Church of Aschaffenburg, just outside of the chapel for which he was to paint the altar. His reputation as an engineer held throughout the last period of his life: in 1527 the City Council of Magdeburg asked the City of Frankfurt for a drawing of the *S 10*

11

famous water-mill, situated on the bridge over the Main River, and the Council of Frankfurt asked Master Mathis to furnish it. Unfortunately the drawing was not executed, because Gruenewald was called upon at the same time, by the City of Halle, again not as a painter, but as "Wasserkunstmacher," i.e., as a builder of fountains. The commission called for an elaborate fountain in the market-place. Gruenewald cannot have done very much in advancing this work since he died in Halle at the end of August, 1528.

The master had left his quiet workshop in Seligenstadt and his office at the court of Mainz in 1525 in a rather dramatic way. The Peasants' War had started in full fury in the Main valley and the burghers of Aschaffenburg, as well as of Seligenstadt, joined the cause of the peasants. When, shortly afterward, Seligenstadt was reconquered by the Archbishop, the painter fled to Frankfurt which proves that he also was on the side of the peasants. Although he was acquitted by the Archbishop he did not resume his service. Among his possessions, which he had stored in Frankfurt when he left for Halle in 1528, were books which clearly prove his leaning towards the ideas of the reformation: a new testament, twenty-seven sermons and many other pamphlets by Luther and "The Twelve Theses of the Christian Faith" appeared as items, when his estate was listed, after his death in the house "Zum Einhorn," by the city authorities. Thus Gruenewald, like Duerer, was an admirer of Luther at heart. It is not surprising that this was so, when one considers that he lived at the court of the Archbishop Albrecht, which stood in the center of the furious controversies of all the leading men of the reformation.

His entire work proves that, right from the beginning, he was destined not to walk in the paths of the official church. He was the heir of the mystics of the fourteenth century. The "Revelationes Sanctae Birgittae," the visions of the Swedish mystic, were published in print in Nuremberg between 1501 and 1502. The story of her most individual relations to Christ and to the Virgin Mary became one of the most important iconographical sources for Master Mathis. Her terrifying realism in describing the Passion of Christ, as well as her luminous glorification of the Virgin Mary were given form and color by Master Mathis' brush.

Two great works which we possess from his last period between 1520 and 1525, the St. Erasmus panel (Munich, Burkhard pl. 63),[6] and the Pietà at Aschaffenburg, his last completed work (Burkhard pl. 66), are representative, the one of the work of the court painter and the second of the work of the follower of the reformation. Both are painted with the same consummate skill. The former is an ostentatious presentation of the Archbishop in the figure of St. Erasmus. The latter is a bold and completely unusual pietà: the dead Christ beneath the mourning hands of the Virgin; she herself is not shown, giving the last strength of expression to the trembling fingers of her hands.

The story of Gruenewald's life, very briefly told, should not mislead us into seeing him as a parallel figure to Duerer or to Leonardo, a man very typical of the time, knowing much, doing more, a painter, an architect, an engineer, a courtier, a revolutionary. In reality Master Mathis was a revolutionary painter only. The admirably comprehensive mind of Duerer approached everything, art and science, with the same earnestness and the same skill. It is in a way comforting to hear of the painter of the Isenheim Altar-piece, that neither the chimney in

12

Aschaffenburg, nor the fountain at Halle really did work. He probably went through all these activities which were expected of him as a great artist, with very little real interest. It is significant that he did not locate his workshop in Mainz, nor even in Aschaffenburg, but for so many years in this little town of Seligenstadt. Thus, after all, Sandrart's story of the lonely man may not be so wrong, in spite of all the activities which the sources relate. His self-portrait, unearthed by Sandrart's eager research, done when he was about fifty years of age and at the height of his career, in about 1515, surely does not show a man of vast worldly ambitions. We can believe that such a man left the court for the sake of the suppressed and suffering. And in its intense inner concentration it is extremely expressive of a great painter. Only in his workshop was he really himself. He never had a school, he never had a real pupil;[7] it even seems that he never had an assistant. Nobody touched his panels but Mathis, the painter.

He is the most exclusive painter we know. Sculpture of his period shows his influence, but no sculptural work can be ascribed to him personally.[8] He never did woodcuts or engravings.[9] He probably hated any kind of reproduction. And he did not want to be restricted to the effect of black and white alone.

EVEN as a draughtsman he was a painter. All his drawings were intrinsically connected with his way of painting. One has well said of him that in drawing he was already painting.

The small number of thirty-six drawings known today cannot be explained by the assumption that he was basically uninterested in drawings. Yet it is—to a certain extent at least—a proof that he was not much interested in preserving his drawings. Quite a few however, which still existed in the sixteenth, seventeenth, or even as late as the early nineteenth century may be lost or only hidden.[10] Thus good fortune may yet increase the number considerably, as it did when the scrap-book of the Savigny collection yielded in 1925, at one time, nine of the most important pieces.

Small as is the number of preserved drawings, it represents a comprehensive cross section of Gruenewald's work, of his aims in his drawings and the use he made of them. In the preparation of paintings there is hardly anything missing, from the most detailed part of a figure-study, to heads, half-figures, entire figures, drapery-studies, figure groups and finally to entire compositional studies. The single figure-studies prevail in number, but considering the obvious losses, this might be quite accidental. One knows that there were surely quite a few most detailed and probably life-sized studies of hands and feet, of which the study for the St. Sebastian of the Isenheim Altar is the only extant example. The last important addition of more recent years is the composition-study for the Virgin of Mercy of the Aschaffenburg Altar. The oil and color spots which it shows suggest its actual use in the workshop during the process of painting. Another composition-study is the Virgin with Christ and the Infant St. John. Quite often the studies of single figures indicate the compositional idea of the whole, not only by the position and action of the figure itself as in the case of the trumpet-player, or of the St. Anthony of the Isenheim Altar, but by the short, sketchy notes of surrounding motifs, proving that the scheme of the entire composition was already fixed to a certain extent; e.g., the addi-

13

tion of the miraculous cloud in the center of the transfiguration or the celestial zone in the study for the Virgin, Queen of Heaven of the Mainz Altar. In some cases landscape setting is indicated, in others a platform-like structure, which apparently was a part of the furnishing of Gruenewald's workshop.

When the plan of a composition was changed, involving changes of single figures, a new study for the same figure may have been drawn, adapting it to the new idea. Thus St. Anthony in the Desert was changed when the idea occurred to introduce the portrait of the donor of the Isenheim Altar in this figure. This case is also one which proves clearly that the master rarely intended to prepare his paintings with a last exactness by drawings; the second St. Anthony study does not show the head of Guersi any more than does the first. In the painting the master used a portrait-study of the head of Guersi which he had already done some time before; and the final execution is quite different from both of these drawings.

If the state of preservation is not responsible, it appears that this rather loose relation between study and execution is most characteristic of Gruenewald's method of drawing in general. The lost original drawing for the Crucifixion of the Isenheim Altar must have been exceptionally close to the executed painting, as the copy still proves. As far as we are able to check, no other figure-study has been taken over exactly into the painting. Sometimes the study is a drapery- and position-study in the first place and the head is only indicated, without expressing much of the idea of the painting: the head of the imposing figure in the drawing for the Crowning of the Virgin is in no way suggestive of that of the Christ-King that must have been intended for the finished painting. Before drapery-studies, studies of nudes may have been made to prepare the position only. But if the assumption is correct that the nude trumpet-player is a study for the Derision of Christ of 1503, it is also an extreme example of the change of position in the final painting. On the other hand, in this case, the negroid type of the face is kept in the execution of the work. If one is able to evaluate the changes between the figure-studies and the paintings it appears that the changes often involve refinement and a greater psychological complexity. The study for the Annunciation of the Isenheim Altar displays simply a terrified withdrawal, whereas the executed figure shows by the face and the gesture of the hands, a very complicated mixture of terror and joy.

This freedom in the relation of drawings and paintings appears more clearly and is at the same time still more enlightening in larger detail-studies of heads and half-figures where one might expect just the opposite. Only one of the preserved examples, St. John the Evangelist, is used with comparatively slight changes in the altar for Tauberbischofsheim. The changes are mostly far-reaching and it is difficult and sometimes doubtful to claim a drawing as a study for a certain painted figure. In this respect the three most effective half-figures of women are very characteristic. Two of them are characterized as figures belonging to a crucifixion, only in a very general way, by their folded hands and the more or less strong upward movement of the heads. Consequently their identification as Mary Magdalen or the Virgin Mary varies considerably. They have the character of studies from life. They may have been drawn without any fixed idea of which character they were finally to represent. One of them, the Winter-

14

thur drawing, was used for a specific figure, in this case for the Virgin of the Isenheim Cruci- *3*
fixion; but this figure was so changed during the actual process of painting that finally only
the hands of the drawing were used in the execution, but these with a rare exactness. Nearer
to the painting is the third of the women's studies, a study for the Magdalen of the Isenheim *5*
Altar, as far as the expression of the face is concerned; however, important changes took place
in the position of the arms.

It is a decisive fact that, for Gruenewald, most drawings were only the noting down of a first
thought, that he never considered them a binding obligation, because it was his deep con-
viction that he would speak his last word in the painting only. Even such a detailed study as
the one for chest, neck and arms of St. Sebastian was changed in one important aspect: when *6, 7*
the painting introduced the strong turn of the head. What finally appears in the painting is *A 13*
always intensified, refined or strengthened; movements are more violent, expressions of grief
or joy are stronger, fingers become longer and finer and so hands much more expressive.
Never losing the connection with the uncompromising realism of the studies, everything is
put on a higher, ideal level of reality. This relative independence gives to the drawings a
precious freedom and a right of their own.

The same is true of the portrait-studies. The Guersi portrait, as well as Gruenewald's self- *8*
portrait, had to undergo extensive changes of position and expression, until they appeared in *9*
this unique confrontation of donor and artist in the figures of St. Anthony and St. Paul of *A 14*
the Isenheim Altar. Two more drawings were certainly made for use in a painting: the
beautiful young woman looking downward is probably meant for a Virgin with the Christ- *24*
child on her lap; the old canon might have been done for a donor figure, to judge from the *36*
raised position of the head and the direction of the eyes. The drawing of Margaret Prellwicz *34*
has no connection with any painting. One day, when visiting the house of her son, Hans von
Schoenitz, whom Gruenewald had met at the court of Albrecht of Brandenburg at Halle,
the painter may have found the old woman sleeping and drawn her portrait without her being aware of it. The unusual pose, caught with the deepest understanding for the unusual
forms, places the drawing in the group of expression studies. The Louvre possesses another *25*
striking example of this kind in the head of the smiling woman. It was also done most probably without any plan for a painting. If it is true that the same face appears in the Oxford *26*
drawing, we obtain some insight into the use of the same model with a change of expression
for different purposes. There are other expression-studies, for instance the two crying angels *22, 23*
which seem to be already rather close to their use in a painting, very possibly for a Mourning
over the Body of Christ. Their remoteness from any model is probably considerable; they
grew out of the master's imagination and his powerful command of the representation of
emotions.

It can easily be understood that the master's interest in expression-studies also caused his
interest in physiognomical representations, as shown in the Three Heads. On the basis of es- *35*
tablished types of wicked and dangerous characters, but yet with a very original power, he *A 25, A 26*
creates a symbol of Antitrinity. It is to be explained most probably as a symbol of Anti-

15

christ,[11] as a powerful indictment of unworthy clerics of his time. There is no way to decide whether the drawing was done in preparation for a special purpose in any painting or only as a reaction to one of the urgent political and religious problems of the reformation.

LOOKING through all the drawings of Gruenewald one receives a striking impression of the consistency of their technique. With only one or two exceptions they are drawn on a similar kind of paper which has a warm tone, between light yellow, yellow-brown, sometimes a somewhat deeper brown. On this prepared paper he draws mostly and basically with black chalk. The absence of scratches in the paper proves that he did not use charcoal and that the chalk was very fine and soft. To that he very often adds, especially in the drapery-studies, the effect of white heightening, using the brush; less often he deepens the shadows with black India ink. In two cases color is added in anticipation of certain color effects of the final execution.

Two rare examples, which by chance were left unfinished, offer a clear insight into the process of the beginning of a drawing: the first is a study for St. Peter, c. 1514-1515, the other, one of the studies of female saints for the Altar of the Virgin Queen of Heaven, c. 1516-1517. After indicating the contour extremely lightly by a very fine and rather unsteady line, he draws layers of shadows, leaving areas of light in the paper tone; then using the thumb or the stump he creates a kind of underpainting on which the more detailed modelling is to be developed. Fortunately, in both cases, finished drawings, belonging to the respective altars, illustrate the final state. From this we can conclude that St. Peter would have been finished in the same way as his beautiful companion-piece, the saint standing in front of a tree, most probably St. Paul. St. Peter would have retained, in general, the harmonious distribution of the larger areas of light and shadows; then the master would have created a strong sculptural effect by varying the shadows in the most refined way; and he would have accentuated the highest light by a strong impasto of white with the brush. At the same time the outline and the interior borderlines of the cloak would have been strengthened, not by making them firm and clear, but by increasing their movement, and partly by duplicating them, showing the lining and the exterior of the material. On the other hand the female saint would have been finished in the style of St. Catherine or St. Dorothy of the same altar, with the same complicated scheme of parallel folds, creating a constantly vibrating change of narrow light and shadow lines. The study for the main figure of this altar, the Virgin in the Clouds, is not to be considered as a finished drawing either, and a similarly complicated linear modelling was to be superimposed on the initial indication of the main areas of light and shadow. Thus on the basis of principally the same underlying modelling, very different final effects could be achieved.

The master uses the same principle in modelling his heads, the faces or other nude parts. Only in very rare cases, a mouth, the form of an eye, the line of an ear or a chin are put in with some linear strength; here also the outlines are mostly extremely thin as well as flexible. The shadows are indicated in rather orderly layers, with preference for a parallel ar-

16

rangement of the single strokes. Sometimes, but certainly not always, they have, by their direction, a form-creating value. More often, they are transposed by wiping into a coherent tone. The studies for the St. Magdalen and the St. Sebastian of the Isenheim Altar are especially clear examples of this use of wiping with the stump. Heightening with white is not usual in the modelling of nude parts. The master used it only in the early drawing of the Crucifixus, which, in other respects, is also unusually detailed; the modelling is done with very fine short strokes, which are not intended to have, by themselves, form-creating value, but constitute an extremely sensitive surface by the finest tonal variety. The free and open manner in which the cross-beam is drawn stands in a very interesting contrast. This same sweeping freedom is displayed also in the drawing of the nude trumpet-player. Sometimes modelling is done with an almost incredible economy. The most perfect example of this kind is the study of the young woman done in preparation for a Virgin Mary and Child. Everything, outline and interior modelling, floats with an airy lightness, and is, while utterly restricted in its means, infinitely rich in its effect.

5, 7 *2* *1* *24*

That this is possible, is due to the incomparable finesse and variation in the use of the chalk, by either pressing more strongly or more lightly. Thus he commands a tone-scale from the deepest black to the most ethereal silvery-gray. If he wants an effect of richness and magnificence the tones are deep and strong. If he wants a sensitive effect, the tones are extremely light and fine. The wealth and warmth of the color of the chalk is always increased by the warm color of the paper,[12] which creates a complete and effective unity of technique and style.

The combination of chalk and yellow-brown paper is so dominantly characteristic of Gruenewald's drawings that only with some difficulty may one acknowledge as work of the master the study for Our Lady of Mercy, drawn with the pen. There is, of course, no doubt that the chalk-drawing was his preferred technique, but it would be completely wrong to exclude, on principle, pen-drawings from his work. Sandrart, relating his visits to the studio of the painter Uffenbach, where he saw the Gruenewald drawings, makes the remark that they were done "mostly in black chalk." This might imply that there were a few others in a different medium. The way in which he uses the pen, in an extremely sweeping manner, is absolutely identical with the outlines of his chalk-drawings. It is a quick catching of the main ideas of form and composition. One may well expect that more of these pen-drawings will some day be found.

33 *1, 20*

THE analysis of Gruenewald's drawing technique is already a part of the analysis of his drawing style. It appears that it is exclusively and utterly a painterly style. Painterly means that the form is created by color; for Gruenewald light and shadow are colors too. In this respect his preserved drawings are completely consistent and as strongly unified stylistically as they are technically.

Therefore it is not an easy task to establish a chronological sequence. Three of the drawings are signed, confirming the stylistic attributions, but none of them is dated. Thus chronology has to be determined connecting the drawings with the paintings, and inserting them

9, 26, 35

into the better established sequence of the paintings. This has been done in the catalogue. The lack of early drawings is a severe handicap in surveying the entire development. The painter of the Munich Derision of Christ, dated 1503, and the somewhat later Basle Crucifixion is already an experienced master of many means. So is the draughtsman of the trumpet-player or the crucified Christ. Whereas examples can be found throughout the whole of the preserved drawings of the former's sketchy manner, the very detailed style of the latter clearly indicates a relatively early period. In spite of the differences both drawings have in common essential features of Gruenewald's style: the sacrifice of harmony and organic logic of form to an extremely characteristic form; the constantly moving outline and moved interior form. Even the detailed modelling of Christ's body is not built up from within, with a real interest in the organic growth, but by the most refined and painterly surface modelling. The trumpet-player's figure with its broad modelling lives almost completely by its outline alone. Comparing this figure with the oboe-player in Duerer's Jabach Altar, which perhaps is its model, one finds decisive differences in the use which both artists made of them: Duerer creates volume and with it depth of space; Gruenewald, turning the figure from its position towards the depth to a position within a plane, creates interesting movement in this plane.

The years from 1508 to 1516, containing the large group of drawings belonging to the Isenheim Altar and to other works executed in the same period, could be characterized as the period of the "rich style." Mostly of monumental size, they display all the aims of the master most brilliantly. The various figure-studies excel in never-ending variations of drapery composition. Eighty years before, Flemish masters like Jan van Eyck, or the Master of Flémalle and in Germany especially Conrad Witz, had discovered the painterly potentialities of these drapery compositions: the possibility of changing colors, tones and values of a color, light and shade ad infinitum. In the angular style of the fifteenth century these form complexes are sometimes in danger of becoming a little schematic. Gruenewald departed completely from the angular style, more radically than even Duerer, combining huge, ponderous motifs and deep shadowy folds with many small motifs, interrupting the direction of the ridge of a fold or seam line unexpectedly, and always varying the form, which is never sharp, but always smooth and versatile, thus uniting grandeur of speech with the finesse of a spirited remark. He loves the wide cloaks of heavy material which allow him greater independence from the body beneath. In fact he cares very little about a clear relation between body and garment. Sometimes it is difficult to decide the exact position of the limbs, yet the drapery arrangement itself is always extremely expressive of the position and action of the respective figures. He changes within the same period the manner of the drapery style, according to the character of the scene. The cloak of the quietly sitting figure of St. Anthony of the Isenheim Altar, belonging to the serene meeting with St. Paul, falls down in rather large, quiet motifs, whereas the excited scene of the Transfiguration is mirrored in the nervous play of many small motifs in the garments of the apostles. The change might be found within the same drawing: the princely mantle of Christ the King is most majestic in the part close to His figure but becomes in the hands of the fanciful angels equally fanciful and animated.

18

It has been said, discussing the master's drawing technique, that all these effects are reached by purely painterly means, excluding almost completely the line drawing. This leads in all details to a transitional effect which might change any minute and gives to the whole an extreme liveliness. It has been mentioned that nearest to the drawings of this period are the grisailles which Gruenewald added to the outside of Duerer's Heller Altar; but it is hardly an exaggeration to say that the full coloristic value and sound of the great figures of all his altar-pieces can be heard already in lower voices in the color harmony of the drawings.

In this harmony is the highest beauty of his work. The strangest forms and the most uncompromising realism are balanced by his never-erring feeling for governing the color scale. The women of the studies for the Isenheim or the Karlsruhe Crucifixion surely are not beauti- *3, 26* ful in a common sense; they have mighty and coarse forms, smooth, round and somewhat flabby. They are conceived without a clear account of the bone structure beneath the skin. But they are of a deeper beauty because of the way light and shade create the forms and play, here more strongly, there more gently over the cheeks, the neck, the nude parts of the shoulder, embuing them with an exciting nearness to life itself. The hair, most richly developed, never becomes an ornamental play and never loses its natural freedom. In modelling the dress, especially the sleeves, the motif of the parallel folds appears for the first time; emphasizing the round form of an arm, they are free of a rigid system, and they combine this purpose with the most spirited change of light and shade.

Of the portraits of this period the head of Guido Guersi, the donor of the Isenheim Altar *8* is more representative than the master's own self-portrait which is altered in its original ef- *9* fect by later overdrawing with the pen. The mighty head of the Prior of the convent of Isenheim illustrates Gruenewald's power of spreading out a wealth of detailed forms yet keeping them under complete control; nothing of the smallest detail is unimportant or lost and yet completely subjugated to the general impression. Thus it combines the most intimate life with the greatest monumentality. The eyes, the nose and the mouth are more distinct and more firm than they are in other portraits, suggesting a rather early date in the beginning of the work on the Isenheim Altar c. 1508-1510.

The power of differentiation of Gruenewald's style within one period is demonstrated by the weeping angel and the young woman, drawn on the front and back of the same sheet of *23, 24* paper; there is no reason to assume that there is any considerable discrepancy between the two. The one, measured by Gruenewald's standard, is an extreme of emotion, the other, an extreme of quiet composure. It is more important to see even here the basic similarities: his power of forming these differences by the same means, with the same effortless ease, and the same unconditional seriousness.

When the Savigny sketch-book was found, some of the drawings which formed a clearly defined stylistic group were rather surprising to those who were used to thinking of the monumentality, the sculptural richness and the realism of those made for the Isenheim Altar. In contrast to them there appears here a strange mannerism. The garments of St. Catherine and *31* St. Dorothy, two studies obviously done for the Altar of the Virgin, Queen of Heaven painted *32* in 1516-1517 for the Cathedral of Mainz, are exclusively composed of narrow parallel folds, changing directions according to the different parts of the dress or cloak. These folds form, especially along the lines of the seams, spirally twisted and shell-like complexes. Looking to Gruenewald paintings one finds that this style begins already in some figures of the Isenheim

A 7, A 12 Altar, e.g. in the drapery of the Magdalen of the Crucifixion, the Virgin in the tabernacle of the Angels' Concert, or the cloak of the Virgin and Child of the same picture. One must recall

3 then that also in the drawing of the Virgin for the Isenheim Crucifixion the sleeves show a similar feature. Thus, what was used in a scattered fashion between 1510 and 1515 becomes a

28 governing style-motif after 1516. The Virgin in the drawing of an Annunciation indicates this development. The motif of the parallel folds is used here more exclusively than in any figure of the Isenheim Altar, yet still more freely, in a less schematized pattern than in the Mainz Altar.

Gruenewald surely had an extremely delicate feeling for the development of style and he was aware of a kind of manneristic revival of linear trends appearing more generally in these

31, 32 years.[13] He embraced this development very quickly, and leading it with full force to a climax,

A 20 he exerted a strong influence over other artists.[14] But one must realize that he himself used the parallel style only in a kind of pseudo-linearism. The possibility of extremely frequent changes from dark to light, of rapidly moving forms was tempting to him. Thus, what appear are vibrating streams of light accompanied by the darkness of the shadows. The scattered examples in the paintings of the Isenheim Altar allow us to reconstruct visually the general impression of the lost paintings of the Mainz Altar: extremely varied in color nuances, extremely movable in all detail forms, just the opposite of a real linear style. Yet the touch of mannerism cannot be denied in the drawings for Mainz, since it appears not only in

32 the drapery style but also in the style of the heads, especially in the inclined head of St. Dorothy in its hyper-sensitive expression.

This mannerism was only a short style interlude in Gruenewald's development and it disappears in the paintings of the last period as well as in the drawings. The late drawings are the direct continuation of those of the period of the Isenheim Altar. They are in many respects so close to each other that the dating of the late group could be a question of debate, if

34, 35 it were not that two of them, the mother of Hans von Schoenitz and the Three Heads have been historically proven to belong between 1520 and 1525.[15] Their style is still more effortless and more unified in the use of painterly modelling; they are less sculptural in detail, and therefore less rich in their general effect; but they are of a quiet monumental greatness which is, in a way, all the more admirable since they are examples of the keenest and most intimate

36 characterization. The portrait head of the old canon also has to be joined to this group as the latest of all the preserved drawings. Being very close to the painted heads of the St. Erasmus panel (Burkhard, pl. 64) it combines the characteristics of the late drawings with the more

1 vigorous open manner used in the earliest period, thus constituting a synthesis of the entire known oeuvre of drawings.

20

THE importance of the drawings in increasing the knowledge and understanding of the master's painted works is considerable. In the cases of the preserved altar-pieces they lead back to the planning state. In discussing Gruenewald's approach to the problem of drawings, and the use of them, it has been said that the painting is always an intensification of the drawing, but usually with considerable changes.

This fact, on the other hand, cautions one against trusting unconditionally to the drawings in reconstructing lost paintings, known only from written sources. One must take into consideration many possible changes. The drawings do not represent more than the planning stage. However, within these limitations, the famous Frankfurt Transfiguration can be reconstructed, in parts at least, combining the two drawings of crouching apostles, one belonging in the lower center, the other to the lower left, with the somewhat hypothetical study of the prophet, either Moses or Elijah, in the upper left. This part of the composition is supplemented by the description of Sandrart who knew the original. He mentions as the most striking features the excitement of the apostles and the miraculous cloud surrounding Christ. The lower region of the cloud is drawn in front of St. Peter, and the reflections of its celestial light play most vividly over the figures of the apostles. Thus, the impression of the color and light miracle of the lost painting, of the agitation of its composition, comparable probably to the Resurrection of the Isenheim Altar (Burkhard, pl. 25) is preserved to a great extent by the drawings.

To a lesser degree, the same may be said of the center-pieces of the Altar of Oberissigheim, the Most Glorious Virgin. However, if the assumption is right that it was a Crowning of the Virgin, and that the majestic kneeling King is a study for the figure of Christ for this same composition, a most unusual representation is foreshadowed by the fanciful figures of the angels and the fantastic motif of the growing trees, filling the old iconographical scheme with a new pictorial spirit.

On more solid ground stands the reconstruction of the Altar of the Virgin, Queen of Heaven for Mainz. Four drawings, again supplemented by Sandrart's description, furnish a rather clear picture of the compositional scheme: the Virgin and Child in Heaven standing on the moon and a group of graceful saints beneath on earth. It appears from the drawings that there were a St. Catherine, St. Dorothy and another unknown female saint, holding a flower. Sandrart remembered St. Catherine, and in addition, St. Barbara, St. Cecilia, St. Elizabeth, St. Appolonia and St. Ursula. Thus a row of at least eight female saints is suggested. Whether or not this *Sacra Conversazione* included male saints remains uncertain. Again the drawings offer, beyond the general arrangement of the composition and the strong impression of the style, indications of the beauty of the color: an apparition in Heaven with all its splendor, the effect of which Gruenewald was eager to forecast by actually adding color to the study for the Virgin.

The most important contribution to a reconstruction of the lost works is the pen-drawing representing the Virgin of Mercy. It is justifiable to assume that it is a study for the lost center-piece of the altar in the Chapel of the Virgin of the Snows at Aschaffenburg, the original frame of which was still in its original place before the war. Reconstruction demonstrates

14, 15

16

15

17

29

31, 32, 30

33

A 24

21

that the composition fits well in proportion and lines to the preserved right wing (Burkhard, pl. 19), showing the miracle of the snows which led to the foundation of Sta. Maria Maggiore. The inscriptions on the frame suggest a combination of the themes of the Virgin of Mercy and the Virgin of the Snows, and the drawing seems to prove that this was also expressed pictorially by including the patrician couple of the snow legend in prominent places beneath the mantle of the Virgin of Mercy. The lost left wing most probably contained another representation of the snow legend.

Some of the drawings prove the existence or the plan for unknown works not mentioned in the preserved sources. The drawing of the Crucifixion in Karlsruhe offers the most important link between the preserved painting at Basle and the Small Crucifixion, thus establishing a most consistent row of crucifixions, culminating in the painting of the Isenheim and the Tauberbischofsheim Altars. The magnificent study of the Vienna saint, perhaps representing St. Paul, and the unfinished study of St. Peter on the reverse side, may point to an altar of St. Peter and St. Paul. Furthermore, there was perhaps a Virgin and Christ-child with St. John, which would constitute the most Italian composition in Gruenewald's works. A Mourning over the Body of Christ is indicated by the studies of two crying angels, and an Annunciation, planned or painted shortly after the Isenheim Altar, by the drawing of the kneeling Virgin. The portrait head of the canon, finally, may point to an unknown late altar-piece; it has been mentioned that the position of the head is that of a kneeling donor figure.

THE drawings of Gruenewald as a whole may appear still more astonishing than his paintings. For these at least one can find a way back to the fifteenth century, to the art of the House-book Master, or to Holbein the Elder. It is quite interesting to note that a contemporary observer was able to see Gruenewald quite well in line with other painters of his time. Melanchthon, apparently intending to name the most important German painters, compares, in 1531, Duerer, Cranach and Gruenewald.[16] "Duerer," he says, "painted everything in a great style, varied by the use of most frequent lines. The pictures of Lucas (i.e. Cranach) are graceful, but, although they are very charming, comparison shows how much they are distant from Duerer's. Matthias' (i.e. Gruenewald) place was in some way in between." Considering that Melanchthon knew best Gruenewald's works in Halle, the Erasmus panel, and perhaps those in Frankfurt and Mainz, but not the Isenheim Altar, and Cranach's graceful Saxonian works and not the exciting early works in Austria, we may say that his classification is quite sensible; and Duerer is surely well characterized by emphasizing his grandeur and his linearism.

Surveying the whole history of painting, one is able to define Gruenewald's work more clearly, as a link between late Gothic and Baroque. The drawings very obviously point ahead. There is hardly anything to connect them with the fifteenth century, and amongst the drawings of the early sixteenth century in the north they are—not isolated—but clearly marked by the uncompromising consistency of their style and the progressiveness of their technique. As a draughtsman Gruenewald surely does not stand between Duerer and Cranach. Cranach is much closer to Duerer than to Gruenewald. Duerer's universal genius was aware of every possibility: there is hardly any artistic means which he did not try in his usual systematic and rational manner. But his striving for harmonious beauty, for clearness and firmness, would always prefer the line as essential means to build up form. For him light and shade remained always complexes of light or dark lines. He uses heightening with white abundantly on bluish or greenish paper in the beautiful studies for the Feast of the Roses, or the Heller Altarpiece, but the whites are applied in clear and regular layers of parallel and crossing lines. Needless to say, his most spectacular achievements in this respect are his copper engravings.

It is perhaps not accidental that Duerer's nearest approach to Gruenewald was in his drawings of 1503 when Gruenewald was painting the altar for the church of Bindlach not far from Nuremberg, and of 1508 when the artists might have met in connection with the Heller Altar. The head of the dead Christ of 1503[17] is near the art of Gruenewald in its extreme expressiveness as well as in its painterly technique. The same is true of the portrait of Conrat Verkell of 1508[18] which is in its irregularity of form quite unusual in Duerer's work. One cannot exclude the possibility of Gruenewald's influence. But even here differences remain. In Duerer's drawings the expressive line still plays an important part, and there is the element of finality in Duerer's drawings, absent in those of Gruenewald. Even when being extremely individual in his characterization Duerer creates a type, whereas Gruenewald even in creating types, as those of the Three Heads, bestows a most individual character on each. This also explains the fact that for Duerer each drawing had a much greater importance than it had for Gruenewald. In his case it was a routine phase in building up a work until a final stage had been reached; a figure or merely a hand or foot was prepared with a last exactness, to be assimilated into the underpainting. In this way the drawing still lives in the painting, whereas in the case of Gruenewald the painting lives already in the drawing, though perhaps in a form different from the one it is ultimately to assume.

The general trend of the early sixteenth century toward a more painterly approach to the form problem appears more clearly in the works of Duerer's pupils Hans von Kulmbach, Hans Schaeufelein or Hans Baldung Grien, but in none of their works as radically as in Gruenewald's drawings. Baldung, sometimes near to Gruenewald in temperament, always differs from the latter's seriousness by a touch of superficial elegance and decorative beauty. The masters of the School of the Danube like Altdorfer or Huber often use outspoken painterly techniques such as clair-obscur, but in their use of chalk they remain nearer to Duerer than to Gruenewald.

In fact one has to look to the south, to Italy, to find more striking similarities. Leonardo's drapery studies and many of his most beautiful heads are close to Gruenewald in artistic means and qualities. He is, of course, like Duerer, in drawing, a man of many methods, but when he departs from forming by lines, and forms by light and shadows, he does so as radically as Gruenewald. In a rare case there appears an even closer relation in spirit: Gruenewald's delicate drawing of the girl's head in Berlin has much of the serene beauty of Leonardo. One is used to seeing Gruenewald as a most typical German painter. That he certainly

23

was, but not in a narrow nationalistic sense. Sandrart expressed this when he called him the "German Correggio." The drawings are the best proof of the international language spoken by Master Mathis.

CATALOGUE RAISONNÉ

1

MALE NUDE, BLOWING A TRUMPET OR A TROMBONE

Black chalk on yellow-brown paper.

271 x 195 mm.

c.1503/04.

Formerly Haarlem, Koenigs Collection.

From the Savigny Collection.

According to E. Winternitz the instrument, the end of which to the right is not visible, is surely a brass instrument, either a trumpet or a trombone. The drawing is perhaps a study in preparation for the *Derision of Christ* (Munich, Alte Pinakothek). This suggestion implies an early date, c.1503. Friedlaender and Feurstein inserted it in the group of late drawings, c.1520, Zuelch in the period of the *Isenheim Altar*, c.1514, before the study for *St. Sebastian* (Nos. 6/7). There is in fact some similarity in the very loose, open and free outline and modelling of the interior forms. But we find already the same manner in the early drawing of *Christ on the Cross* (No. 2), not in the modelling of the body, where apparently a much more detailed representation of the interior forms is intended, but very much so in the treatment of the upright cross-beam drawn in the same sweeping way.

The type, the action and position of the nude bear out the interpretation that it was prepared as one of the figures surrounding Christ in the mocking scene. Musical figures belong to the general iconography of this scene. Compare, e.g. Duerer's woodcut of the *Small Passion* (B. 30), or a drawing c.1410, Erlangen, Univ. Lib., Bock pl. 6, 11, where one man is blowing a trumpet into the ear of Christ. Adversely, this view from the rear is similar to the oboe-player in Duerer's *Derision of Job* of the *Jabach Altar* (fig. A2), leading us to suppose that Gruenewald saw that work in Duerer's workshop in 1503, while work-

ing on the altar for Bindlach, not far from Nuremberg, now in Lindenhard (Burkhard pl. 1). When he began the *Derision of Christ* shortly afterwards, he may have planned to place the Trumpet-player, drawn from the rear, in the foreground. But he rejected this idea, keeping the figure of a torturer leading Christ away, which is more common in this place, putting the musician in the rear to the left instead, now with a fife and a drum (fig. A1). Yet the figure in the painting has still some connection with the drawing, having also a rather negroid face and similar hands. When Gruenewald painted, c.1515, the *Bearing of the Cross* (Burkhard pl. 59), where these figures drawn from the rear also appear quite often, he avoided it deliberately. This confirms the early date of the drawing. One can say that in general this type of figure belongs to the compositional type of the 15th, rather than the 16th century.

Lit.: facsimile: Friedlaender, *Savigny Drawings;* Friedlaender, No. 28; Zuelch, No. 16; Burkhard, No. 22; Feurstein, p. 144.

2

CHRIST ON THE CROSS

Black chalk; original heightening by brush with white only partly preserved; cut out around the cross-beams and body and pasted on lighter paper; on yellow-brown paper.

531 x 320 mm.

c.1504/05.

Karlsruhe, Kunsthalle.

Later inscription on the substitute paper: *Holbein deli [neavit] M P.* Modern inscription: M. Gruenewald to the right. The drawing was found in the Print Room of Basle by Curator Koelitz.

Gruenewald's painted *Crucifixion* in the Basle Museum (fig. A5), c.1504, the earliest we know, is the closest in time to this drawing. The position of the body, particularly, is related in important features, which are changed in the *Small Crucifixion,* c.1506 (formerly Haarlem, Koenigs Collection; fig. A6). The body, later moved to the right, hangs just in front of the heavy vertical beam as in the Basle work. The head is bent to the left, and is not yet the formal center of the whole composition as it becomes later, beginning with the *Small Crucifixion.* Furthermore, the feet are nailed to the cross symmetrically, as in the Basle work, whereas in the *Small Crucifixion* both are twisted to the right in the same direction. Besides, the outline of the upper part of the body is very similar to that in the *Basle Crucifixion.* Yet it is not likely that this drawing is a study for the latter: there are new features. The more powerful head and crown of thorns point ahead to the *Small* and to the *Isenheim Crucifixion* (fig. A7). The horizontal beam, made of two pieces, displays an advance in a realistic treatment. The expressive curved form appears for the first time.

The fact that the nails are not shown excludes the possibility that the drawing is a copy of an existing painting since lost. The extremely fine quality justifies its being considered an original study for a painting, not executed or now lost, between the *Basle* and the *Small Crucifixion.* Schmid, and following him, Friedlaender, both conjecture that it was a study for the *Isenheim Altar,* a possibility confuted by its much closer connection with the Basle work. Nevertheless, Zuelch is surely wrong to date it before the Basle painting. Burkhard's doubt as to whether it is a Gruenewald drawing at all has no serious justification.

In cutting out the cross and figure, parts of the contour were damaged: the right side of the breast and loincloth, the outline of the left arm and left hand, and the body underneath the left arm. The copy at Basle (fig. A3), made before the drawing was cut out, affords some possibility of reconstructing the original at these points.

Lit.: facsimile: Ges. f. Z. K.; Friedlaender, No. 6; Schmid, p. 256; Zuelch, No. 2; Burkhard, No. 23; Schoenberger, *Staedeljahrbuch* II, 1922.

3

STUDY OF A WOMAN BENEATH THE CROSS, USED FOR THE VIRGIN MARY OF THE CRUCIFIXION OF THE ISENHEIM ALTAR

Black chalk on yellow-brown paper.

403-414 x 297-302 mm.

c.1510.

Winterthur, Oskar Reinhart Collection.

Formerly Licht Collection.

From the Savigny Collection.

Study after a model, used in preparation for the first version of the Virgin of the *Isenheim Altar.* We know that this figure was changed very much during the actual process of painting (see Schmid, p. 134). In the early plan Mary, with eyes not closed, was to stand erect, unsupported by St. John. This drawing is primarily connected with that stage, i.e., at first Mary's rôle was to be more active, more in accord with the figure of the Baptist, and perhaps similar in attitude to the Virgin of the *Basle Crucifixion.* After the motif of the fainting Virgin was introduced (fig. A7), only the hands, with the fingers in exactly the same position, were used in the final version of the painting (fig. A10).

Burkhard connects the drawing with the St. Magdalen of the *Isenheim Crucifixion,* but I cannot follow him. Zuelch is wrong to suggest a connection with the Virgin of Duerer's *Heller Altar.*

Lit.: facsimile rep.: Friedlaender, *Savigny Drawings;* Zuelch, No. 9; Burkhard, No. 33; Schoenberger, in *Beitraege zur Geschichte der deutschen Kunst,* I, 1924, p. 164; C. Koch, *Zeichnungen Altdeutscher Meister zur Zeit Duerers,* Dresden, 1922; Burkhard, p. 69.

4

STUDY FOR A WOMAN BENEATH THE CROSS OF CHRIST

Black chalk; torn triangular section of upper forehead and hair of original restored; on yellow-brown paper.

384 x 283 mm.

c.1510.

Berlin, Kupferstich-Kabinett.

Formerly Luetzschena, Speck von Sternburg Collection.

On the reverse side of No. 5.

This drawing belongs to the same period as the one in the Reinhart Collection (No. 3). Drawn on the same paper, and similar in style, it is also a study after a model in preparation for the *Isenheim Crucifixion*. The position of the hands suggests the Virgin more than St. Magdalen.

Lit.: facsimile rep.: Ges. f. Z. K.; Friedlaender, No. 8; Zuelch, No. 8; Burkhard, No. 25; Felix Becker, Zwei neue Gruenewald Zeichnungen, in *Zeitschrift fuer Bildende Kunst*, N F 25, 1914, p. 275; Schoenberger, *Beitraege zur Geschichte der deutschen Kunst* I, 1924, p. 164.

5

STUDY FOR THE ST. MAGDALEN OF THE CRUCIFIXION OF THE ISENHEIM ALTAR

Black chalk, wiped in the shadows; torn section of left eye, part of forehead of original renewed; on yellow-brown paper.

384 x 283 mm.

c.1510.

Berlin, Kupferstich-Kabinett.

Formerly Luetzschena, Speck von Sternburg Collection.

On the reverse side of No. 4.

The steep angle at which the head and eyes are raised is appropriate to a figure kneeling, rather than one standing, beneath the cross, and therefore is probably a study of St. Magdalen. The open neck of the garment is consistent with a usually more worldly appearance. Although the costume is changed in the painting, the figure remains sufficiently similar in both expression and position to identify the drawing specifically as a study for the St. Magdalen of the *Isenheim Crucifixion*. The

fingers also are in exactly the same position (fig. A12). As was his custom, in the painting Gruenewald strengthened the accents by throwing the head backward more violently, and by extending the arms forward to point toward Christ. Compare the similar changes in the relation of the Winterthur drawing (No. 3) to the painted Virgin of the *Isenheim Altar* (fig. A10).

Lit.: facsimile: Ges. f. Z. K.; Friedlaender, No. 7; Zuelch, No. 7; Burkhard, No. 26; F. Becker and G. Schoenberger as in No. 4.

6–7

STUDY FOR HANDS AND ARMS OF ST. SEBASTIAN OF THE ISENHEIM ALTAR

No. 6.
Black-gray chalk on yellow-brown paper.

238 x 189 mm.

c.1514.

Dresden, Kupferstich-Kabinett.

On the reverse side of No. 11; originally belonged to the left of No. 7, later separated by cutting apart; study from life of hands and lower arms for the St. Sebastian of the *Isenheim Altar* (fig. A13). The painting was done c.1514, which establishes the date of the drawing.

No. 7.
Black-gray chalk, wiped in the shadows, on yellow-brown paper.

279 x 195 mm.

c.1514.

Dresden, Kupferstich-Kabinett.

Formerly Goettingen, Ehlers Collection.

On the reverse side of No. 10; originally belonged to the right of No. 6; study from life of chest and upper arms for the St. Sebastian of the *Isenheim Altar*. Dated like No. 6 (fig. A13).

Approximately 15 mm. of original missing between No. 6 and No. 7.

Both formerly Leipzig, Gottfried Winkler Collection.

This study of a nude does not show the cloak added in the painting. On the right half appears a slight trace of the neck and chin in full profile, indicating that the abrupt turn of the head which appears in the painting was not planned when the study was made. The contour shows various *pentimenti* to gain a more varied outline, which is retained in the painting. In the painting the fingers are longer, finer, and more expressive than they appear in the drawing. The drawing is perhaps one of those Sandrart saw (Source 17) in the possession of Phillip Uffenbach: "very beautiful drawings, done mostly in black chalk; some almost life-size."

According to the inscription on the drawing it was in the collection of Gottfried Winkler, Leipzig, in the early nineteenth century, from which it was sold in auction in 1815. The catalogue mentions eleven drawings of Gruenewald: of these six are studies of hands, two studies of feet.

Lit.: facsimile rep.: Ges. f. Z. K.; Friedlaender, No. 12, 13; Schmid, p. 277; Zuelch, No. 17, 18; Burkhard, No. 17, 18; First published by Lehrs in *Mitteilungen aus den Saechsischen Kunstsammlungen* I, 1910.

8

STUDY FOR THE HEAD OF AN OLD MAN, PROBABLY GUIDO GUERSI

Black chalk, heightened slightly with white on the left side; on light yellow paper.

341 x 253 mm.

c.1508/10.

Weimar, Schlossmuseum.

The man represented is thought to be the Prior of the Convent of Isenheim, Guido Guersi, who commissioned the paintings of the *Isenheim Altar*. This identification depends on a similarity to the head of St. Anthony as it was finally executed in the painting (fig. A14), with a change in the position of the figure from right to left and from three-quarter to half-profile; compare No. 11, which first indicates the plan of the donor portrait. There are in fact fundamental similarities in the structure of the powerful head, the nose and mouth, the setting of the eyes. The style of the drawing fits that of the studies of women for the *Crucifixion,* particularly the one now in Winterthur (No. 4). Bock, who first published the drawing, emphasizes the fine, rich detail in both drawings. The portrait probably was done between 1508 and 1510 during the early stages of preparation for the *Isenheim Altar,* without a set plan for where it was to be used. This would account for the change in position and consequent reversal of profile.

Lit.: Friedlaender, No. 15; Zuelch, No. 15; Burkhard, No. 32; Elfried Bock, *Jahrbuch der Preussischen Kunstammlungen* 46, 1925.

9

SELF-PORTRAIT WITH DRAW-ING-QUILL

Black chalk, heightened with white by brush; strongly retouched later by pen; on brown paper.

206 x 152 mm.

c.1514-15.

Signed 🜨

Erlangen, Universitaets-Bibliothek.

Date 1529 added later.

A list of twenty-five German artists of the 16th century was inscribed in ink on the reverse side at the beginning of the 17th century. "Mathis von Aschaffenburg" appears as sixth in this list.

The drawing is very badly preserved, but without doubt was, in its original state, a Gruenewald drawing. It was used by Sandrart for his second portrait of Gruenewald in his *Teutsche Academie,* Part III, pl. 4 (fig. A18). He obtained it from Ph. J. Stromer of Nuremberg, and published it believing that it showed the master in his old age more perfectly than the one he had used previously in the first volume. (See Part II, pl. CC.) He published it, according to his own words, "in honor of the famous German Correggio." (Source 18) Zuelch mentions that a certain Dr. Heinrich Stromer was court physician to Albrecht von Brandenburg and possibly a relative of the Nuremberg Stromer family, suggesting that through this connection the drawing might have come into the possession of Ph. J. Stromer. Sandrart himself executed a copy of the drawing (fig. A17), which he used as the basis for his engraving. The Erlangen drawing has assumed special importance because the first engraved portrait is now rejected since Winkler published (see Bibliography) the original drawing used for this engraving. Sandrart had mistaken for a drawing of Gruenewald by Duerer a drawing of an unknown man, done in 1522 by Wolf Huber (R. von Hirsch Coll., Basle). The Duerer monogram which led Sandrart astray is a later addition.

The drawing shows the painter with a quill in his right hand and must have been drawn by using two mirrors. It served as a study for the head of the Hermit St. Paul of the *Isenheim Altar* (fig. A16), but in the painting the features are changed to indicate a much older man. This entitles us to date the drawing in the period of the later sections of the *Isenheim Altar*, c.1514-1515. In turn this date is most important, because the drawing representing the man as of at least fifty years of age compels us to assume that Gruenewald was born c.1465. Moreover, the monogram *MG*, has an original background in the same chalk as the drawing. Before it was retouched the monogram was surely quite similar to that on the drawing of the Three Heads (No. 35), where it is preserved completely untouched. Zuelch suggests (p. 381) that the drawing also might have been used once more, since the Frankfurt painter, Jacob Marrel, left among his possessions in 1681 "eines Aschaffenburger malers eigen Conterfait," i.e., "the self-portrait of a painter of Aschaffenburg;" this might have been an inscription like the one of fig. A15.

Lit.: facsimile rep.: Schmid, Pl. 46; Zuelch, No. 14; E. Bock, *Zeichnungen der Universitaet-Bibliothek Erlangen*, Frankfurt, 1929, p. 24; R. A. Peltzer, *Sandrarts Teutsche Academie*, 1925; Wilhelm Fraenger, *Matthias Gruene-*

wald, *Ein physiognomischer Versuch*, Berlin, 1936.

10

STUDY FOR ST. ANTHONY THE HERMIT OF THE ISENHEIM ALTAR

Black chalk, heightened with white by brush; on yellow-brown paper.

279 x 195 mm.

c.1514.

Dresden, Kupferstich-Kabinett.

Formerly Goettingen, Ehlers Collection.

In the 16th century inscribed *Isnaw* in the upper right corner.

On the reverse side of No. 7; originally on one sheet with No. 11.

The drawing shows the saint during his visit to St. Paul in the desert (fig. A14). With his right hand slightly raised he is looking upwards in the direction of the miraculous appearance of the raven. According to Schmid (p. 267), in the painting the head also was originally raised in this manner. Thus this is surely the earlier of the two preserved studies of this figure. At this stage it was not yet Guenewald's intention to represent the donor Guido Guersi in the person of the Saint. The place on the rock where the donor's coat of arms appears later is still covered by growing grass. The inscription *Isnaw*, i.e., Isenheim in the upper right corner is one of the few early evidences that Gruenewald worked there. The drawing was ascribed once to Wolgemut and attributed to Gruenewald first by Konrad Lange.

Lit.: facsimile: Ges. f. Z. K.; Friedlaender, No. 10; Schmid, p. 267; Zuelch, No. 19; Burkhard, No. 19.

11

STUDY FOR ST. ANTHONY THE HERMIT OF THE ISENHEIM ALTAR

Black-gray chalk, heightened with white by brush; on yellow-brown paper.

238 x 189 mm.

c.1514.

Dresden, Kupferstich-Kabinett.

On the reverse side of No. 6; originally on one sheet with No. 10.

The drawing represents the second state of the figure of St. Anthony visiting St. Paul in the desert. In this later version the saint does not look up toward the raven, but straight forward in the direction of St. Paul. This is the more usual arrangement of the scene in the 15th century: e.g., the tympanum of the Church of St. Anthony, Frankfurt-on-Main, c. 1415; the painting by the Master of Basle of 1445, Donaueschingen, Gemaeldegalerie. The primary reason for this change was probably the decision to represent the donor of the paintings, Guido Guersi, in the figure of the saint. This is indicated by the position of the hands, now in the usual gesture of a donor, and by the empty space in front of the rock, to be filled in later with the donor's coat of arms. The portrait-study of Guido Guersi in Weimar (No. 8) shows the head in the same three-quarter profile as in this study, but with right and left reversed.

Lit.: facsimile rep.: Ges. f. Z. K.; Friedlaender, No. 11; Schmid, p. 262; Zuelch, No. 20; Burkhard, No. 17; Lehrs, in *Mitteilungen aus den Saechsischen Kunstsammlungen* I, 1910, p. 41; G. Schoenberger, Das Portalrelief der Antoniterkirche zu Frankfurt a.M. in *Im Frankfurter Raum* I, 1931.

12

STUDY FOR THE VIRGIN MARY OF THE ANNUNCIATION OF THE ISENHEIM ALTAR

Black chalk on brownish paper.

160 x 146 mm.

c.1511/12.

Berlin, Kupferstich-Kabinett.

From the Savigny Collection.

This drawing has been proved a preparatory study for the Virgin of the *Annunciation* of the

Isenheim Altar (fig. A11) by the arrangement of a chest, partly covered by the Virgin's cloak, on which the Scriptures with the prophecy of the Annunciation are reverently placed. Moreover, in the head and garments of the drawing there is a general similarity to the painting, done 1511-1512, which fixes the former's date. There is an important difference, however, in the attitude of the hands and in the position of the head. In the drawing the head is bent back more sharply, and the hands are clasped and kept near to the body, indicating the Virgin's astonishment and terror upon being confronted with the appearance of the angel and with the message borne to her. In the painting, however, the head is bent backward a little less, and the face expresses the transition from terror to joy. This intermediate state is most expressively illustrated by the attitude of the hands, which now are more outstretched, and seem to hesitate between rejection and submission.

Lit.: facsimile: Friedlaender, *Savigny Drawings*; Friedlaender, No. 14; Zuelch, No. 12; Burkhard, No. 3.

13

GARMENT STUDY FOR A CROUCHING FIGURE OF THE TRANSFIGURATION (?)

Black chalk on yellow-brown paper.

130 x 180 mm.

c.1512.

Collection of Mr. and Mrs. LeRoy M. Backus, Seattle, Washington.

From Oppenheimer Collection, London. Formerly L. Grassi Collection, whose collector's mark appears in the lower right corner.

Later inscribed: *A. Durer* in the lower right-hand corner.

It is difficult to make out beyond doubt the position of the figure in this study. Most probably it is meant to be a study for a figure facing the right, completely covered by a large cloak. It is seen from the side, cringing, with the hidden left knee bent, and the right leg, in front, stretched out backward. Because of the attitude of the figure this study is usually linked with the lost *Transfiguration*, an explanation which has more probability than any other. However, Zuelch is not right in connecting it with the figure of the apostle which we have to assume at the right side of the group. It belongs, if at all, to the figure at the left, for which we also have the study (No. 15) usually identified as St. Peter. In contrast to the latter, here only the rear parts of the garment are executed with great exactness; the feet are completely hidden beneath the cloak; in the front part of the figure the supporting right arm is just indicated, and the head is omitted, or else it was meant to be completely covered by the cloak.

Lit.: Friedlaender, No. 1; Zuelch, No. 6; Burkhard, No. 10.

14

STUDY FOR A KNEELING APOSTLE OF THE TRANSFIGURATION OF CHRIST

Black chalk, partly wiped in the shadows, heightened with white by brush; on white paper, colored yellow-brown for the drawing.

146 x 208 mm.

c.1512.

Dresden, Kupferstich-Kabinett.

Inscribed *frankfurt* in the upper left-hand corner by a 16th-century hand.

The study was for the lost *Transfiguration*, which, according to Sandrart (Sources 17, 18), Gruenewald painted "in water-color" for the Dominican Church of Frankfurt-on-Main. The place of the painting was to the right above Duerer's *Heller Altar*. The connection of the drawing with that work is documented by the inscription *frankfurt*, done by the same 16th-century hand as the inscriptions on Nos. 10 and 29. Stylistically the drawing is between the study for the *Annunciation* (No. 12) and the St. Anthony studies for the *Isenheim Altar* (Nos. 10 & 11).

Thus the year 1512 can be suggested, a date which is supported by a document (Source 1) mentioning Gruenewald's presence at the Dominican monastery at that time. The strong foreshortening in the attitude of the figure suggests that in the painting it was supposed to be in or near the center, i.e., it was the central figure of the three apostles witnessing the miracle. Of the many attempts to see in the work of later artists the echo of Gruenewald's lost *Transfiguration,* only the one of Zuelch has some probability, namely, the stucco relief in the Mausoleum of Philipp III of Hesse, in the Stadtkirche of Butzbach, done in 1618 by Christian Steffan after drawings by Uffenbach. (See Lit.)

Lit.: facsimile rep.: Ges. f. Z. K.; Friedlaender, No. 2; Zuelch, No. 5; Burkhard, No. 15; Schmid, pp. 263-265; *Kunstdenkmaeler im Grossherzogtum Hessen* III, 2 pl. III.

15

STUDY FOR A KNEELING APOSTLE (PETER?) OF THE TRANSFIGUR-ATION OF CHRIST

Black chalk, partly wiped in the shadows, heightened with white by brush on white paper, colored yellow-brown for the drawing.

148 x 263 mm.

c.1512.

Dresden, Kupferstich-Kabinett.

Along with Nos. 13 and 14 the study belongs to the lost *Transfiguration* of the Dominican Church at Frankfurt-on-Main. Because of the tonsure the figure is usually identified as St. Peter. Like No. 13 it is a study for the left-hand figure of the group of three apostles witnessing the transfiguration and is probably the later version of the two. This is indicated by the decisive turn of the figure to the right, where the miraculous cloud appears, out of which God speaks (St. Matthew 17:5): "This is my beloved Son in whom I am well pleased." According to the same text "a bright cloud overshadowed" the apostles; here, as in many famous representations, the cloud has settled down upon the group. (Compare Raphael's *Transfiguration* in the Vatican Gallery.) According to Sandrart (Source 17) the cloud was one of the striking features of Gruenewald's painting.

Lit.: facsimile rep.: Ges. f. Z. K.; Friedlaender No. 3; Zuelch, No. 4; Schmid, pp. 263-265; Burkhard, No. 16.

16

FRAGMENT OF A STUDY OF A KNEELING MAN WITH RAISED HANDS

Black chalk, heightened with white by brush; the sleeves and parts of the garments were overpainted later with red; on yellow paper.

235 x 165 mm.

c.1512.

Berlin, Kupferstich-Kabinett.

In the second half of the 16th century the drawing was cut out along the contour and pasted on a new sheet of paper to fit into a larger setting. An empty inscription tablet was added at the left, and below, an inscription of Psalm verses on the fear and love of God. (See reproduction in Ges. f. Z. K.) The most recent restoration, in the Berlin Print Room, eliminated the later additions, but left the retouching of the original with color done along with the resetting.

The figure has not been satisfactorily interpreted. Schmid, and, among others, Zuelch, call it a scorning Pharisee for an *Ecce Homo*; this is not supported by the expression of the face. There is the same difficulty with Friedlaender's explanation, which takes the figure to be a disputing Pharisee in a representation of *Christ among the Doctors*. Hagen, who connected the drawing with the *Founding of Sta. Maria Maggiore* from the *Altar of Mary of the Snows* in Aschaffenburg (now in Freiburg i. Br.), identified the figure as the one in the middleground, the patrician John, who has the vision of Mary in the sky. But that figure is sitting on the steps of the palace, with only the left arm raised. Feurstein, and following him, Burkhard, added this drawing to the studies for the lost *Transfiguration*, believing it to be an apostle. The

drawing is certainly the nearest in style to the studies established as belonging to this work (Nos. 14, 15), and must be placed in the same period. If it was done in planning the *Transfiguration*, it might be asked whether it is a preparatory study for the left-hand figure of either Moses or Elijah, the two prophets, who always appear in the sky to the left and right of Christ. The pointing gesture of the hands has been traditional for these figures since the Romanesque period; compare, e.g., the *Otto Gospels* (Munich, Staatsbibliothek, lat. 4553). Sometimes the prophets are represented kneeling, as in the painting of Daddi (Florence Academy); compare also the small figures of the prophets on the Tabernacle of the *Angels' Concert* of the *Isenheim Altar*, which are very similar in gesture and style. The composition of the lower part of the garment is more appropriate to a figure hovering in mid-air than to one kneeling on solid ground. The beardless face, which does not belong to the usual iconography of either Moses or Elijah, might be explained as having been taken directly from the model, the drawing being primarily a garment and position study.

Lit.: Friedlaender, No. 4; Schmid, p. 261; Zuelch, No. 3; Hagen, pp. 190, 193; Feurstein, p. 138; Burkhard, No. 1, and p. 70.

17

STUDY OF CHRIST FOR THE CORONATION OF THE VIRGIN OF THE ALTAR OF OBERISSIGHEIM

Black chalk, heightened with white by brush; on yellow-brown paper.

286 x 366 mm.

c.1515.

Berlin, Kupferstich-Kabinett.

On the reverse side of No. 20.

Formerly von Radowitz Collection.

The crown and sceptre or sword clearly indicate the kneeling figure as a king; the globe further justifies the identification of the figure as Christ. In the study of St. Dorothy (No. 32) the Christ-child is signified by the same attribute. The composition suggests a central figure on the podium to the right. This consideration, the gesture of the right hand and the angels supporting the garments make the interpretation of the drawing as a study of Christ for a *Coronation of the Virgin* more probable than any other. Hagen, Fraenger and Weser propose it as a study for an *Adoration of the Magi,* but the angels would be out of place in such a work. Kehrer and Friedlaender consider the figure an angel for an *Annunciation,* but this too is not supported by the usual iconography of this scene. To consider it for a *Coronation of the Virgin* still leaves us with the difficulty of explaining the setting of trees, since the scene is usually represented as taking place in heaven. However, one may recall the *Mary in the Garden on the Crescent* by the Master of Flémalle (Brussels, Muller Collection), where the Virgin is placed in an earthly landscape. The drawing fits best stylistically in the period of the late sections of the *Isenheim Altar* (fig. A14) and of the *Madonna of the Veil* for Tauberbischofsheim (now in Stuppach; No. 26). In this period we can assume at least preparatory work for the *Altar of Oberissigheim,* donated by Heinrich Reitzmann in his last will of 1514 where the center-piece of the Altar is entitled: "the most glorious Virgin," (Source 2) which well might have been applied to a *Coronation of the Virgin.* The altar either was never executed or is lost.

Lit.: facsimile: Ges. f. Z. K.; Friedlaender, No. 24; Schmid, p. 258; Zuelch, No. 23; Burkhard, No. 10; Fraenger, p. 147; Feurstein, p. 141; Hagen, pp. 162, 218; Kehrer, in *Forschungen zur Kirchengeschichte,* Leipzig, 1932, p. 211; R. Weser, Der Bildgehalt des Isenheimer Altar in *Archiv. f. Christliche Kunst,* Vol. XL, 1926, p. 7.

18

UNFINISHED STUDY FOR ST. PETER

Black chalk on yellow-brown paper.

368 x 296 mm.

c.1515.

Vienna, Albertina.

On the reverse side of No. 19.

The attribute in the left hand of the saint is usually considered to be a key; he is identified therefore with St. Peter. Compare the note to No. 19, where the study of the standing saint, on the reverse side is tentatively identified as St. Paul, which might have been planned as a companion-piece for the same altar. Meder, however, considers the drawing to be a study for the standing St. Anthony of the *Isenheim Altar,* with the gesture of the left arm, and the arrangement of the cloak changed. His assumption that the attribute is only a part of St. Anthony's staff, the rest not being drawn in, is not very convincing; neither is his assumption that the saint is wearing a close-fitting cap like that of St. Anthony. However, since there is in fact a certain similarity with the St. Anthony painting, Zuelch may be right in supposing that the painter also used this or a similar drawing for the stationary wing of the *Isenheim Altar,* which was painted c. 1515. (fig. A9)

Lit.: facsimile: Ges. f. Z. K.; Friedlaender, No. 27; Zuelch, No. 22; Burkhard, No. 31; Meder, in *Die Graphischen Kuenste,* Vol. XLIII, 1920.

19

STUDY FOR A SAINT (ST. PAUL?) IN FRONT OF A TREE

Black chalk, strongly heightened with white by brush; on yellow-brown paper.

368 x 296 mm.

c.1515.

Vienna, Albertina.

On the reverse side of No. 18.

The aged saint is standing in front of the trunk of a tree with wide-spread roots. There is no agreement about the saint's identity. His characteristics and attributes are as follows: he is old, bearded and bald, and barefooted; a wide cloak covers an undergarment with a high collar; he wears a belt for his sword, the handle of which appears at his left hip, a long staff leans in the crook of his left arm; his hands are clasped in front of his breast in a praying gesture. Usually the saint is said to be either St. Joseph or St. Jerome. St. Jerome is mentioned as having been the figure on the left wing of the *Altar of Oberissigheim* (Source 2): the Vienna saint has in fact a very close affinity of style and motif to the study for the Altar's center-piece, the Christ-King for the *Coronation of Virgin* (No. 17). But since the sword is not an attribute of St. Jerome, this identification, which I formerly shared myself, has to be abandoned. Yet the connection is important for dating the Vienna drawing c. 1515. St. Joseph has been mentioned by those who interpret the Kneeling King as belonging to an *Adoration of the Magi*; here, too, the sword is not appropriate. If we consider the possibility that the drawing represents an apostle, the type of head, the beard, the baldness and the sword all would be appropriate to St. Paul. In that case, however, the staff would be unusual. On the reverse side of this drawing is an unfinished study of St. Peter (No. 18). Was there a planned or executed altar showing St. Peter and St. Paul? In this connection one should mention the engraving of the Master H L, the sculptor of the *Breisach High Altar,* which represents St. Peter in front of a very similar (fig. A20), and unusual stump of a tree. The style of this print is related to that which Gruenewald developed shortly after the Vienna drawing was done, while he was preparing the *Altar of the Virgin* in the Cathedral of Mainz, c.1516 (Nos. 28, 29, 30). Was this print done, perhaps, with knowledge of the painted St. Peter, the companion piece of St. Paul, which might have been more advanced in style in the manner of the Mainz Altar?

Lit.: facsimile: Ges. f. Z. K.; Friedlaender, No. 26. Schmid, p. 270; Zuelch, No. 21; Burkhard, No. 30; Schoenberger, in *Beitraege zur Geschichte der deutschen Kunst,* I, 1924.

20

STUDY FOR THE VIRGIN WITH CHRIST-CHILD AND THE INFANT ST. JOHN THE BAPTIST

Black chalk on yellow-brown paper.

240 x 174 mm.

The oval form is due to the way the drawing was matted, and has nothing to do with the composition itself.

c.1515.

Berlin, Kupferstich-Kabinett.

Formerly von Radowitz Collection, the collector's mark of which appears in the lower left-hand corner, along with the stamp of the Berlin Kupferstich-Kabinett.

On the reverse of No. 17.

In spite of the rather unclear character of this rapid sketch, some parts of which may have been rubbed off, the representation can be considered to be the following: The Virgin is sitting, shown in three-quarter length, with the Child on her lap in vigorous movement; the lower part of His body is moved to the right, the left leg hanging down; the position of the right leg is not clear; the head of the Child is inclined to the left, and with both hands He holds a head of a lamb on His mother's lap; the Virgin's right hand, holding the Child on her lap, lies below; the body of the lamb was not drawn in or has been rubbed away. The figure of the infant St. John the Baptist in the rear fits the motif of the lamb. He holds a staff in his right hand in front of Mary's shoulder, supposedly a cross-staff, the cross not being shown. In obvious symbolism he is presenting the cross-staff to the Virgin, who grasps it with her left hand. This composition and iconography are decidedly not northern, but lead us into the realm of the Italian High Renaissance. This, as well as the details of the composition, e.g., the strong movement of the Child's body across the body of the Virgin, suggest that Gruenewald knew of works in the manner of Leonardo's *St. Anne*, transmission of which by a print is very improbable in this particular case. Thus this sketch is an important document, suggesting a journey by the painter to Italy. The drawing belongs in the period when the painter was working on the *Isenheim* and *Oberissigheim Altars*. It was not done for either of these works, but for an unknown painting c.1515. Wind has classified the drawing with representations of Charity, having been misled by the work's indeterminate character. But he bears out our point in stressing the Italian character of the work.

Lit.: facsimile: Ges. f. Z. K.; Friedlaender, No. 25; Schmid, p. 259; Zuelch, No. 24; Burkhard, No. 11. Edgar Wind, *Charity*, in *Journal of the Warburg Institute*, Vol. I, 1937-1938.

21

STUDY FOR THE VIRGIN OF THE VEIL IN TAUBERBISCHOFSHEIM, NOW IN STUPPACH, PARISH CHURCH

Black chalk; the brocade ornaments on the dress in brown by brush; on light yellow-brown paper.

314 x 278 mm.

c.1515/16.

Berlin, Kupferstich-Kabinett.

From the Savigny Collection.

The general position of the Mother and Child, the motif of the Virgin presenting a fruit to the Child, the motif of the tree at the right all clearly connect the drawing with the Altar which is now in the parish church of Stuppach (fig. A21). I follow Feurstein in his conjecture that this painting was not the center-piece of the *Altar of Mary of the Snows* at Aschaffenburg (see note to No. 33), but was done for an *Altar of the Virgin of the Veil* at Tauberbischofsheim. In the painting the beautiful Veil, a famous relic of the church of Tauberbischofsheim, is added. On the other hand, the crown of Mary in the drawing is omitted in the painting. Another difference between painting and drawing is in the gesture of the Child, which in the drawing is just a realistic gesture of acceptance, but has in the painting the higher significance of both receiving and blessing. The style is near to that of the studies for Oberissigheim (No. 17) and for the Vienna saint (No. 19), to which it is also linked by the tree motif.

Lit.: facsimile: Friedlaender, *Savigny Drawings*; Friedlaender, No. 23; Zuelch, No. 25; Burkhard, No. 9; Feurstein, p. 141.

22

HEAD OF A CRYING ANGEL WITH WIDE-OPEN MOUTH

Black chalk, heightened with white by brush; on light yellow-brown paper.

244 x 200 mm.

c.1515/16.

Berlin, Kupferstich-Kabinett.

Allowing for the change from joy to grief, stylistically and as far as the types are concerned, this study, and its companion piece, No. 23, are very close to the angels of the *Angels' Concert* of the *Isenheim Altar*, the section executed somewhat earlier c. 1514-1515. They are done for an unknown representation of the *Mourning over the Body of Christ*, or perhaps for a *Martyrdom of Saint Sebastian*, or some similar scene. It may not be accidental that two woodcuts of Hans Baldung, the *Martyrdom of Saint Sebastian* (B. 37) and the *Dead Christ Carried to Heaven by Angels* (B. 43), show similar crying and weeping angels although of a more conventional character. Especially the second may reflect a lost work of Gruenewald. The interpretation first given by Guenther (see Lit.) and adopted by Zuelch, which explains the drawing as a study for the head of the young man, guide to a blind hermit who is attacked by robbers, painted for the Cathedral of Mainz has to be rejected; 1520, the date of this altar which we know from a copy by Uffenbach, now lost (Zuelch, p. 340), is too late; furthermore there are physiognomic reasons against such an explanation.

Lit.: Friedlaender, No. 31; Zuelch, No. 26; Burkhard, No. 14; Fraenger, p. 107; Guenther, *Das Martyrium des Einsiedlers von Mainz*, Mainz, 1925.

23

HEAD OF A WEEPING ANGEL

Black chalk on light yellow-brown paper.

276 x 196 mm.

c.1515/16.

Berlin, Kupferstich-Kabinett.

35

The monogram *MG* in the lower right corner is a later addition.

On the reverse side of No. 24.

Along with No. 22 this drawing is connected in style with the angels of the *Angels' Concert* of the *Isenheim Altar*. It is also an angel's head for a *Mourning over the Body of Christ*, or for a *Martyrdom of Saint Sebastian* (see note to No. 22). Here too, explanations as a "crying man" or "torturer in a Passion scene" must be rejected.

Lit.: facsimile: Ges. f. Z. K.; Friedlaender, No. 30; Zuelch, No. 27; Burkhard, No. 13; Hagen, *Gruenewald*, pp. 20 and 210.

24

HEAD OF A YOUNG WOMAN

Black chalk on light yellow-brown paper.

276 x 196 mm.

c.1515/16.

Berlin, Kupferstich-Kabinett.

On the reverse side of No. 23.

Study from life of a young woman. The arrangement of the hair has caused discussion: some critics suggest that it may be a man wearing a close-fitting cap. This is not true. The girl wears braids around her head, fixed by a small band or net; and also the costume with open neck is clearly that of a woman. The study probably was made c.1515 for a seated Virgin and Child. But neither the *Isenheim Madonna* nor the one of the *Tauberbischofsheim Altar* (now Stuppach) are sufficiently similar to identify the study with one of them. The motif of the strongly inclined head, which suggests the Child on her lap, is against its being a portrait study proper. Zuelch's assumption that the drawing is a study of one of the saints of the *Altar of Mainz* of 1516 (Nos. 29-32), is not convincing, because the type is not yet the manneristic one of that altar, but is connected more closely with the studies of women for the *Isenheim Altar* (Nos. 3 and 4).

Lit.: facsimile: Ges. f. Z. K.; Friedlaender, No. 29; Schmid, p. 260; Zuelch, No. 28; Burkhard, No. 12.

25

HEAD OF A SMILING WOMAN

Black chalk wiped in the shadows; slight touch of red on the cheeks; on white, only slightly yellowish paper.

201 x 147 mm.

c.1515/16.

Paris, Louvre, Cabinet des Desseins.
In the upper left corner Duerer's monogram, added later.

Collection mark of Robert de Cottes in the upper left-hand corner.

Collection mark of Coypel at right above the shoulder.

A shawl, draped like a turban, covers the hair and forehead almost down to the eyes, as customarily worn by women bathing. The throat and shoulders are bare. The face bears a close resemblance to that of the study for the Virgin at Oxford (No. 26). Zuelch even suggested that both were done from the same model; this possibility should not be excluded, but it is not beyond some doubt. At least one can say that the drawing, by its wealth of plastic forms and intense expressiveness, links the studies for the Crying Angels (Nos. 22, 23), and even the Winterthur woman (No. 3) with the Oxford drawing. Thus a date between the *Isenheim Altar* and the *Tauberbischofsheim Crucifixion* (now in Karlsruhe) is probable. The drawing has been placed in a later period, c.1520, by Friedlaender, but the late head studies, like the Mother Schoenitz (No. 34), or the Stockholm canon (No. 36) achieve the same wealth of forms by even more delicate, painterly means. The drawing was published by Lippmann as a Duerer (*Duerers Handzeichnungen*, Vol. III, No. 306); ascribed to Gruenewald first by Schmid and Friedlaender. (See Lit.)

Lit.: facsimile: Ges. f. Z. K.; Friedlaender, No. 32; Schmid, p. 269; Zuelch, No. 11; Burkhard, No. 28. M. J. Friedlaender, in *Repertorium fuer Kunstwissenschaft*, Vol. XXVIII, 1905.

26

STUDY FOR THE VIRGIN BE-
NEATH THE CROSS, PERHAPS
FOR THE HOLY CROSS ALTAR
AT TAUBERBISCHOFSHEIM
(NOW IN KARLSRUHE)

Black chalk, the shadows of the face partly wiped; on yellow-brown paper.

380 x 240 mm.

c.1515/16.

Signed at the left: [m]athis.

Oxford, University College.

Inscribed by pen at the right, c. 1600:
*Disses hatt Mathis von Ossenburg des Chur-
fuersten [von] || Mentz Moler gemacht || und
wo du Mathis ge || schriben findest das ha[t]
Er mit Eigner hand gemacht*

At the left, in a 17th-century hand: *matsia*
a wrong transposition of the original signature.

This study is the cornerstone for establishing the *oeuvre* of the Gruenewald drawings,
because the original signature *mathis* is
confirmed and explained by the inscription
at the right, which most probably is in the
hand of Phillip Uffenbach, c. 1600. In this
respect I do not share the doubts of Schmid.
Uffenbach owned, according to Sandrart (see
Source 17), many drawings by Gruenewald.
The inscription reads: "This is done by
Mathis von Ossenburg [i.e., Aschaffenburg],
the painter of the Elector of Mainz, and
where you find written *mathis*, that he did by
his own hand." Opinion as to the date of the
drawing varies considerably: Schmid and
Hagen date it late, after 1520. I placed it, at
first, with the drawings made for the *Isenheim
Altar* (see Lit.). This was accepted by Zuelch.
However, Schmid (see Lit.) upholds the late
date, adding that the drawing was done as a
study for the *Karlsruhe Crucifixion* (fig. A8).
While this may be true, and rather extensive
changes in the execution of the painting are
possible, one must emphasize that the *Karlsruhe Cruciifxion* is not so late as is usually suggested, i.e., after 1520, but is most probably

not later than 1515-1517. Feurstein (pp. 113,
120), and after him Zuelch (p. 330), mention
a donation in 1515 for the *Altar of the Holy
Cross* of the church of Tauberbischofsheim
(the original location of the Karlsruhe painting), by Pastor Virenkorn, who also belonged
to the clergy of Aschaffenburg, and certainly
knew Gruenewald. The earlier date for the
Karlsruhe Crucifixion is supported by an ob-
servation by Phyllis Bober, that the study
could also have been used, with a change of
expression, for the St. Magdalen of the *Magdalen Altar* of Isenheim, painted before 1516,
and preserved only in a copy at Donaueschingen. Besides, the drawing is surely connected in style with the one in Winterthur
(No. 3), with the Crying Angels (Nos. 22, 23),
and with the *Smiling Woman* of the Louvre
(No. 25), which most probably was executed
from the same model. All these drawings are
not later than 1515-1516. (See also note to
No. 25.) The Oxford drawing was published
first in 1904 by M. A. Sidney Colvin.

Lit.: facsimile: Ges. f. Z. K.; Friedlaender,
No. 21; Schmid, p. 268, and also the article
Gruenewald, in the *Thieme-Becker Kuenstler-
Lexicon;* Hagen, p. 208; Zuelch, No. 10; Burkhard, No. 27; Feurstein, pp. 113, 120; Schoenberger, in *Beitraege zur Geschichte der deutschen Kunst*, I, 1924; Friedlaender, in *Repertorium fuer Kunstwissenschaft*, XXVIII, 1905.
M. A. Sidney Colvin, *Selected drawings from
old masters in the University Galleries and the
library at Christ Church, Oxford*, Part 2, 1904.

27

STUDY FOR ST. JOHN THE EVAN-
GELIST OF THE HOLY CROSS AL-
TAR AT TAUBERBISCHOFSHEIM,
NOW IN KARLSRUHE

Black chalk on yellow-brown paper.

434 x 320 mm.

c.1515/16.

Berlin, Kupferstich-Kabinett.

From the Savigny Collection.

Study for the upper body of the St. John of
the *Karlsruhe Crucifixion* (fig. A8). This painting was done for Tauberbischofsheim, and

was perhaps donated by Pastor Virenkorn for the *Altar of the Holy Cross* in 1515 (see note to No. 26). The painting is copied more faithfully from the drawing than is usually the case in Gruenewald's work: see, for example, the torn parts of St. John's jacket. However, there are additions, like the coat and the more heavily bearded chin, and changes, like the omission of the moustache, the Evangelist's generally older appearance, and especially the change from the serious but somewhat indifferent expression of the model to an outspoken expression of grief. Similarly the expression of the hands is strengthened, by making the fingers longer, finer, and more sensitive.

Lit.: facsimile: Friedlaender, *Savigny Drawings;* Friedlaender, No. 22; Zuelch, No. 35; Burkhard, No. 8.

28

VIRGIN OF AN ANNUNCIATION

Black chalk, heightened with white; the shadows strengthened with black India ink by brush; on yellow-brown paper.

207 x 210 mm.

c.1516.

Berlin, Kupferstich-Kabinett.

From the Savigny Collection.

By its composition the drawing is connected to a certain extent with the study for the *Annunciation* of the *Isenheim Altar* (No. 12). As in that study the Virgin's dress is spread out under the book. But in the Isenheim study there is a chest, which is replaced here by a cushion and a low platform. (Compare Nos. 17 & 32.) Moreover the rich and most spirited use of parallel folds proves that the drawing is later than the *Isenheim Altar,* where this style appears, but only occasionally. Thus the style of the drawing points ahead to the *Altar of the Virgin* of the Cathedral of Mainz of 1516-1517 (Nos. 29-32), where it becomes the dominant feature. Thus Feurstein, Zuelch, and Burkhard are wrong to include the drawing in the studies for the *Isenheim Altar.* After the *Mainz Altar* of 1516-1517 the style of the parallel folds was no longer used.

Therefore the study must have been made for a painting between the *Isenheim* and *Mainz Altars* which is now lost or was never executed.

Lit.: facsimile: Friedlaender, *Savigny Drawings;* Friedlaender, No. 14; Zuelch, No. 13; Burkhard, No. 4; Feurstein, p. 140.

29

STUDY FOR THE VIRGIN, QUEEN OF HEAVEN, OF THE ALTAR FORMERLY IN THE CATHEDRAL OF MAINZ

Black chalk, with slight retouching with India ink. The full moon, the clouds, and the adjoining parts of the Virgin's garment in yellow watercolor wash; on yellow-brown paper.

323 x 268 mm.

c.1516/17.

Vierhouten, Van Benningen Collection.

Formerly Haarlem, F. Koenigs Collection. From the Savigny Collection.

Exhibited New York World's Fair, 1939; Smith College, 1945.

Inscribed in a 16th-century hand, in the upper right corner: *menz.*

The Virgin is characterized as the Queen of Heaven by the crown, and by the scepter in her right hand; the Christ-child holds the imperial globe with cross; both are bending down toward the left; the Virgin, hovering in the air, is surrounded by shining clouds, with the full moon beneath her feet. The inscription *menz* (i.e., Mainz) indicates that the study was done for one of the altars which, according to Sandrart (see Source 17), Gruenewald did for the Cathedral of Mainz. A winged altar, it showed in the center: "Our Lady with the Christ-child in the cloud; below, on earth, are reverently standing many saints displaying remarkable gracefulness." Studies for three of them are preserved (Nos. 30-32). The representation of the Virgin as Queen of Heaven on the moon is drawn primarily from the *Apocalypse,* chapter 12: "And there appeared a great wonder in heaven: a woman clothed with the sun, with the moon under her feet, and upon her head a crown of twelve stars." Near to Gruenewald's workshop in Seligenstadt was a stained glass window in the Stadtkirche of Hanau, upon which is represented the crowned Virgin with Child on the Crescent (fig. A23), done c.1500 by an artist of the School of the House-book-Master, who was also Gruenewald's most important teacher and did a print on the same topic (L27). Possibly there existed an earlier representation of this theme by Gruenewald himself, preserved only in a rather weak woodcut copy done c.1600, but signed with a monogram *MG*, and with the date 1510 (fig. A22). To the compositional type of the Mainz Altar, with the upper and lower regions, the Virgin in heaven, and the assembly of saints on earth, compare Titian's Altar of 1523 of Rome, Vatican Gallery (originally in the Frari Church of Venice) which may be cited as a specifically related form of the *Sacra Conversazione*. Gruenewald's knowledge of this type may have been derived from his acquaintance with Italian works (see note to No. 20). In this connection one should remember Sandrart's curious designation of Gruenewald as "the German Correggio" (Source 18), probably conceived in front of such a work as the *Mainz Altar*, with its graceful saints. However, the apocalyptic features are stressed in the German work. We know that Gruenewald's work for the Cathedral of Mainz was begun in 1516, and that he painted three altars for Mainz; also that the one which was painted in 1520 showed the martyrdom of a saint in a landscape (Source 17). Since the style of the *Virgin, Queen of Heaven*, which appears more fully executed in the studies for the female saints (Nos. 31 & 32), is very different from the style of the known late works, like the *Saint Erasmus* panel of 1522-1523 (Munich, Pinakothek), or the late *Pietà* of 1524-1525 (Aschaffenburg, Stiftskirche), the *Queen of Heaven* must have been painted at the beginning of the work for Mainz, i.e., in 1516-1517.

Lit.: facsimile: Friedlaender, *Savigny Drawings;* Friedlaender, No. 17; Zuelch, No. 32; Burkhard, No. 21; Stephen Kayser, The Madonna Queen of Heaven in *Parnassus,* October, 1939; Max Lehrs, *The Master of the Amsterdam Cabinet,* 1893-1894.

30

UNFINISHED STUDY OF A FEMALE SAINT FOR THE ALTAR OF THE VIRGIN, QUEEN OF HEAVEN, FORMERLY IN THE CATHEDRAL OF MAINZ

Black chalk on yellow-brown paper.

316 x 215 mm.

c.1516/17.

Berlin, Kupferstich-Kabinett.

From the Savigny Collection.

On the reverse side of No. 31.

The figure of the saint, holding a flower in her right hand, is an unfinished study for one of the saints of the *Mainz Altar* who stand beneath the *Virgin, Queen of Heaven*. Its unfinished state is very revealing of the way Gruenewald began a drawing by building up forms from the very start in an extremely painterly way, almost completely without lines, by means of complexes of light and shadow. The unfinished state of this drawing is all the more illuminating, since it is probable that in completing the drawing the painter would have added the rich and complex play of the parallel folds of the garment, to be seen in the drawing of St. Catherine (No. 31), which is quite similar in the basic arrangement of the garment, or in the drawing of St. Dorothy (No. 32), both studies for the same altar. The flower indicates that this may be another study for St. Dorothy, or possibly for St. Elizabeth.

Lit.: facsimile: Friedlaender, *Savigny Drawings;* Friedlaender, No. 20; Zuelch, No. 31; Burkhard, No. 7.

31

STUDY FOR ST. CATHERINE OF THE ALTAR OF THE VIRGIN, QUEEN OF HEAVEN, FORMERLY IN THE CATHEDRAL OF MAINZ

Black chalk, heightened with white by brush; on yellow-brown paper.

316 x 215 mm.

c.1516/17.

Berlin, Kupferstich-Kabinett.

From the Savigny Collection.

On the reverse side of No. 30.

In her right hand St. Catherine is holding the sword of her martyrdom; in her left, the sword-belt and her cloak, which, thrown over her right arm, hangs down in front in heavy folds. She wears the crown of her martyrdom, and her head is encircled by a large radiant double halo. A somewhat rocky terrain is indicated at her feet. The study belongs to the lost *Altar of the Virgin, Queen of Heaven,* painted c.1516-1517 for the Cathedral of Mainz. (See Source 17 and note to No. 29.) There appear in the upper part at the right and left indications of the clouds in which the Virgin was represented above the assembly of saints (see No. 29). The general composition and detail of the garment are an extreme example of the use of narrow parallel folds. Originally a feature of the female costume of the period (e.g., see Duerer's Drawing of a Nuremberg Woman of c. 1495, L. 187, Panofsky, *Duerer,* fig. 59), it was used by Gruenewald as a means of developing an excited play of strongly agitated lines of light and shadow. See the note to the Virgin of an Annunciation (No. 28), which, in this respect stands between the *Isenheim* and *Mainz Altars.* In the *Mainz Altar* the style is at its climax in forming twisted and shell-like complexes with a kind of manneristic overemphasis. A brief phase for Gruenewald, soon disappearing almost completely from his work, this style was further developed in the Upper Rhine region, between 1520 and 1525 by the Master H L, the master of the *High Altar of Breisach.* Compare also the master's engravings: e.g., *St. Peter* (fig. A20 and note to No. 19). There are also drawings of 1518-1520 by Holbein the Younger for stained glass windows, which show the influence of this style. A drawing of the Virgin and Child, done in Holbein's workshop (fig. A19), is so near in the detail of the drapery to the Gruenewald drawings for Mainz that

one may surmise a lost work by Gruenewald as model. Compare also the form of the crown, which is like a circle of feathers, with the crown of the kneeling Virgin in the tabernacle of the *Angels' Concert* of the *Isenheim Altar* (Burkhard, pl. 24).

Lit.: facsimile: Friedlaender, *Savigny Drawings;* Friedlaender, No. 19; Zuelch, No. 30; Burkhard, No. 6; Ganz, *Die Handzeichnungen Hans Holbeins, d. J.* XX, 2; Schoenberger, Review of Friedlaender, Die Zeichnungen Gruenewalds der Sammlung Savigny in *Oberrheinische Kunst* I, 1925-1926.

32

STUDY FOR ST. DOROTHY OF THE ALTAR OF THE VIRGIN, QUEEN OF HEAVEN, FORMERLY IN THE CATHEDRAL OF MAINZ

Black chalk, heightened with white; the shadows strengthened with India ink by brush; on yellow-brown paper.

358 x 256 mm.

c.1516/17.

Berlin, Kupferstich-Kabinett.

From the Savigny Collection.

In her left hand the saint holds a basket or dish for flowers; in her right, a flower. The Child to her left, identified as the Christ-child by the globe on which He stands, is presenting a pear to her. According to her legend, although it was then winter, Christ brought her a basket of fresh fruit and flowers on the way to her execution. The saint is standing on a platform similar to that appearing in Nos. 17 & 28, apparently a piece in the painter's workshop. The head of the saint is encircled by a radiant halo. Beyond any doubt the drawing belongs to the *Mainz Altar* (see note to No. 29). This most refined example of the manneristic period of the painter shows at their height not only the extremely varied form of the use of parallel folds, but also, in the gracefully bent head, a sweetness which foreshadows the Virgin of the *Altar of Niederrothweil* of 1526 by the Master H L.

Lit.: facsimile: Friedlaender, *Savigny Drawings;* Friedlaender, No. 18; Zuelch, No. 29; Burkhard, No. 5; Schoenberger, review of Friedlaender, Die Zeichnungen Gruenewalds der Sammlung Savigny in *Oberrheinische Kunst,* I, 1925-1926.

33

STUDY FOR OUR LADY OF MERCY
OF THE ASCHAFFENBURG
ALTAR

Pen on paper, in some parts slightly strengthened in the shadows by brush wash. Pasted on another sheet of paper.

309-315 x 204-231 mm. (irregular).

c.1515/16.

Stockholm, National Museum.

Oil and color spots indicate the use in the workshop.

The Virgin, a scepter in her right hand, is standing on the serpent which turns to the body of Adam, covered by a shroud, outstretched beneath the group. Her cloak, spread wide and supported by angels, protects the pope and dignitaries of the church at the left, the emperor and representatives of the secular classes at the right. To the left is the kneeling figure of a woman, to the right, near the emperor, a kneeling man, best identified as the patrician John and his wife, who founded Santa Maria Maggiore. Above are three flying angels with sword, bow and arrows; thus—as also in other examples of this theme (see Lit.)—motifs of threatening heavenly punishment in the Last Judgment are included. At the top, in the center, is the figure of God the Father with right hand raised and the globe in His left, the Dove of the Holy Ghost beneath. The entire group is hovering in the air.

Schilling has assembled detailed evidence of the connection between the motifs of the drawing and established works of Gruenewald to prove his authorship. But it should be emphasized also that the very rapid, somewhat casual manner of drawing conforms exactly with the chalk drawings of Gruene-

wald like the *Virgin with the Infant St. John* (No. 20) or the study for *St. Sebastian* (Nos. 6 & 7).

As to the purpose, Schilling is right that the drawing is a study for the lost center-piece of the altar of the chapel dedicated to the Virgin of the Snows in the Collegiate Church of Aschaffenburg. The right wing, showing the *Miracle of the Snows* is preserved in the panel, now at Freiburg i. Br. (Augustiner-Museum) (fig. A24). The panel with Virgin and Child now at Stuppach, claimed by Schmid to be the center-piece of the altar, definitely must be excluded. (See note to No. 21.) The text of the inscriptions around and in the lunette of the original frame of the missing center-piece (see Sources 3, 4), preserved *in situ,* is most appropriate to the theme of *Our Lady of Mercy;* the inscriptions were partially renewed but without any change in the original text. They have no connection whatsoever with the *Adoration of the Magi,* painted in 1577 by Isaac Kiening, which has been in the frame since the original was removed. The first inscription around the arch reads: "Mary, Mother of grace, Mother of mercy, protect us from the enemy" (Source 3). From the several last wills of Canon Reitzmann one can conclude that the center panel was a donation of Caspar Schantz, who is mentioned together with Reitzmann in the inscription of the final dedication of the altar in 1519 (see Source 8). Probably it was already in place when the chapel and the altar were consecrated in 1516 (Source 5). This date is conceivable for the drawing, which, even in its sketchy state, displays manneristic features similar to those of the drawing for the *Altar of the Virgin, Queen of Heaven,* of the Cathedral of Mainz, done in 1516-1517 (compare No. 32). The frame was originally designed without wings, which were an addition of 1517-1518 (see Schmid, p. 202). It seems certain therefore that Reitzmann must have agreed to join his donation of 1513 and 1514 (see Source 2) to that of Schantz, thereby linking the theme of the Virgin of Mercy with that of the Virgin of the Snows, as the inscription in the lunette indicates: "Dedicated to Mary, the Holy Virgin of the Snows. Pious Mother, with your peaceful eyes watch over the mortals whose fate is torture of many kinds" (Source 4).

This juxtaposition of themes is perhaps also indicated by the presence of the patrician John and his wife, of the Virgin of the Snows legend, in the crowd protected by the Virgin of Mercy. As to the composition, it can be said to be in better harmony with the preserved right wing of the altar now in Freiburg than with the *Madonna* now in Stuppach, formerly claimed as center-piece. The size and proportion of the figures are the same, and the group of kneeling figures on the right side of the center-piece is well followed up by the kneeling figures of the donors on the wing, which lead to the figures in the middle and background of the panel (fig. A24). The representation on the lost left wing is not known.

Lit.: Edmund Schilling, Eine Federzeichnung des 16. Jahrhunderts und ihre Beziehung zu Gruenewald, in *Staedeljahrbuch*, Vol. IX, 1935. V. Sussmann, Maria mit dem Schutzmantel, in *Marburger Jahrbuch fuer Kunstwissenschaft*, Vol. V, 1929.

34

PORTRAIT OF MARGARET PRELLWITZ, THE MOTHER OF HANS VON SCHOENITZ, SLEEPING

Black chalk, slightly heightened with white by brush. The entire face later done in flesh tone by brush; on yellowish paper. 288-287 x 224-227 mm., cut irregularly. c.1522/23.

Paris, Louvre, Cabinet des Desseins.

Unknown collector's stamp of the period of Napoleon III.

On the reverse is a cursive inscription: *margret brellwitzin.* Above, in capitals by another hand: *HANS SCHENECZ MUOTTER, AETATIS SUAE* 71 . . . , (Zuelch dates both inscriptions 1520-1530).

The drawing was rightly ascribed to Gruenewald by Baumeister (see **Lit.**). Previously Tietze had attributed it to Master J Z (see Lit.), but had also mentioned that Gruenewald's name was suggested in connection with the drawing. Officially it had previously been called: *Ecole du Danube.* Demonts called it, in the Louvre Catalogue of 1937: "Manière de Matthias Gruenewald." The attribution to Gruenewald is best made certain by comparing the study with other late drawings, like the Three Heads (No. 35). It is on the same level of effortless modelling of complicated forms by the most refined painterly means. In addition, the person represented was connected with the circle of the court of Archbishop Albrecht of Brandenburg at Halle. Margaret Prellwitz was the third wife of a citizen of Halle, Martin Schoenitz, and the mother of Hans von Schoenitz, counsellor to Albrecht from 1520 on. His portrait by Conrad Faber (Sigmaringen, Collection of the Castle) shows a definite family resemblance to the old woman. In 1522-1523 Gruenewald painted the *Saint Erasmus* panel (now Munich, Alte Pinakothek) for the Neue Stiftskirche at Halle; in that work the heads show the same ripeness of style, another indication that the drawing was done in the same period.

Lit.: Zuelch, No. 36; Engelbert Baumeister, Eine Zeichnung Gruenewalds, in *Muenchner Jahrbuch, Neue Folge* III, 1926 (with good reproduction); H. Tietze, in *Burlington Magazine*, Vol. XLIV, 1924; Demonts, *Inventaire général des desseins des Ecoles du Nord*, Vol. I, 1937; Rolf Huenecken, Gruenewald in Halle, in *Zeitschrift fuer Kunstgeschichte*, Vol. V, 1936; F. von Marcuard, *Das Bildnis des Hans von Schoenitz*, Munich, 1896.

35

THE THREE HEADS

Black chalk; shading partially wiped; on light yellow-brown paper.

272 x 199 mm.

c.1523/24.

Signed ᛗ on the lower edge.

Berlin, Kupferstich-Kabinett.

Most important because of the authentic signature. Three heads of characteristically different types are represented, with separate necks but joined by the back part of the heads, in a tripartite unity, which is also stressed by the encircling halo as well. This halo also precludes interpreting the heads as just physiognomic studies. All critics have finally agreed that a kind of trinity is meant, the Holy Trinity quite often being represented by a tripartite head. Compare, e.g., fig. A27 (*Schwabenspiegel*, c.1400, Vienna, Hofbibliothek, 2780). There too the three heads are surrounded by a halo.

In attempting to explain the drawing we must determine: 1. the general scientific and artistic realm to which it belongs; 2. its specific meaning.

1. The drawing surely belongs to the class of physiognomical representations. The characteristic differences of the three faces are not merely accidental, but follow an established iconography of physiognomical types. There we find, with slight differences but basically the same, the face of a very energetic type, like the one in the center of the drawing, with strong forehead, keen eyes, strong nose, thin mouth, and powerfully protruding chin. A second type, with receding forehead and protruding eyes, often bald, with thick nose and lips, and receding chin, is like the face at the left. A third, which is rather in between the first two, is often similar to the one at the right. We come upon these types again and again in Leonardo's physiognomical studies. Compare, for example, in fig. A25 the face at the left with Gruenewald's center face, the one at the right with Gruenewald's left. Similar types can be found in the woodcut illustrations by Hans Baldung Grien, made for Johannes de Indagine's *Introductiones in Chiromantiam, Physiognomian*, etc., Strassburg, Schott 1522. The examples reproduced from that work are taken from a reprint, Paris, 1543. Compare fig. A26, lower right, with Gruenewald's center head; fig. A26, lower left with the left; and fig. A26, upper right with the right.

It is noteworthy that Gruenewald surely knew Johannes de Indagine very well: he too belonged to the court of Albrecht of Mainz. When he published the book in 1522 Indagine was dean of the Collegiate Church of St. Leonard in Frankfurt, close to Seligenstadt where Gruenewald had his workshop. Thus it might well be that Gruenewald's interest in this kind of physiognomical studies was aroused, and his knowledge of the common pattern of physiognomic iconography increased by the publication of Indagine's book, most probably known to him immediately after it appeared.

2. Among the many scholars who discuss the drawing (see Lit.) there is no agreement as to the meaning of the *Signum Triciput*. It must be admitted that to the present no explanation has been given which is convincing beyond any possible doubt. The votes are divided even about the fundamental question of whether the forces represented are devilish and evil or divine and good. Lately Benesch advocated a kind of real Trinity, formed against the background of the Peasants' War: ". . . the heads in all their ugliness . . . filled with holy expression, like the apostles of the rebellious artisans and peasants . . . over whom the spirit came and made them rise." This is, of course, a completely personal hypothesis, without confirmation in the sources. Wind's most recent attempt at a more neutral explanation must also be rejected. He suggests a study for an altar of St. Anne. The three heads would then represent the three husbands of St. Anne, shown in representations of the Holy Kinship in a close group. But even the example which Wind finds most comparable (Cranach, Vienna, Academy) is strongly different from the tripartite unity of Gruenewald's drawing. I hold that one should rely primarily on the judgment that the left face clearly represents an evil character, which—since the unity of the three hardly can be doubted—also implies that the somewhat ambiguous status of the other two is to be considered as on the immoral side. One cannot say that Gruenewald relied primarily on Indagine's book. The latter's interpretations are also sometimes ambiguous, uniting evil and good traits in one figure. Yet some of his interpretations can readily be applied to Gruenewald's types. For example, Indagine says of his weak, fat type (fig. A26, lower left), which is to be compared with Gruenewald's left face: "Those whose eyes protude calf-like out of their forehead are dull and stupid, sensual, lying and lazy. But those whose eyes

are deep-set and fixed as if on a goal are cruel, and tryants. . . . A very pointed nose marks a tyrant. (This applies to Gruenewald's center face.) An open mouth (Gruenewald's left face) signifies the shameless, the deceiving and sensual. . . . If the skin on the upper part of the nose be not smooth and even, a profane, false, and choleric [character] is signified (Gruenewald's right face, Indagine, fig. A26, upper right)." (Source 9.) If we acknowledge that evil characters are intended in the drawing, the most probable of all the given explanations is that which places the drawing among the representations of an antitype of the Holy Trinity, i.e., a trinity of the devil, a concept going back to Origen (in his *Commentarium in Epistolum ad Romanos*, V, 562). Panofsky kindly allowed me to use a note from a forthcoming study in which he will point to the fact that in the *Bible Moralisée*, and its derivations from the 13th to the 15th century, Satan usually appears three-headed with a radiant crown (fig. A28) having the special significance of Antichrist. From the list of possessions left to his heir (see Source 13) we know that Gruenewald was familiar with Luther and his ideas. In response to the Pope's ban, Luther, just after the year 1520, likens the Papacy to the kingdom of Babylon and to the Antichrist. In this connection a letter published by Zuelch (p. 405), which Johannes de Indagine wrote to his Lutheran friend Johann Braunfels of Mainz in 1522, i.e., the same year in which his book on physiognomy was published, assumes importance. It criticizes strongly the evil clergy: "Who does not hate us [i.e., the clergy] with good reason? . . . Who would have believed that such an high title [i.e., canon] would be connected with such an *indolent and lazy negligence* [left face?], *such indulgence of the passions* [center face?], *such a criminal life* [right face?]." Thus the *signum triciput* of Gruenewald with its deceiving halo of sanctity instead of a radiant crown is perhaps a Protestant antithesis of the Trinity, a pictorial pamphlet characterizing the unworthy clergy in general as Antichrist, giving to the older concept of the trinity of the devil a political significance. Mackert (see Lit.) also proposes an antipapal explanation.[19]

The date of the drawing can readily be es-

tablished stylistically, the closest in that respect being the portrait of the mother of Hans von Schoenitz (No. 34), done c.1522-1523, and the portrait of an old cleric (No. 36), which also belongs to this late period. The extremely rich, differentiated and completely smooth modelling of the drawing also can be compared with the late paintings, especially with the late *Pieta*, done in 1524-1525 for the Collegiate Church of Aschaffenburg. Thus the style suggests a date for the *Three Heads* shortly after the appearance of Indagine's book, i.e., c.1523-1524.

Lit.: facsimile: Ges. f. Z. K.; Friedlaender, No. 5; Zuelch, No. 33; Schmid, pp. 45 and 258; Burkhard, No. 2; Hagen, p. 212; Feurstein, p. 33; Guenther, *Das Martyrium des Einsiedlers von Mainz*, 1925, p. 46; E. Panofsky, Signum Triciput, in *Studien der Bibliothek Warburg* XVIII, 1930; A. Hakel, *Die Trinitaet des Boesen*, Dissertation Heidelberg, 1931; E. Mackert, Trias Romana. Zur Deutung einer Gruenewaldzeichnung, in *Westdeutsches Jahrbuch fuer Kunstgeschichte*, 1943; Otto Benesch, *The Art of the Renaissance in Northern Europe*, Cambridge, 1945; Edgar Wind, Sante Pagnini and Michelangelo in Gazette des Beaux Arts Ser. VI, Vol. XXVI, 1947.

36

HEAD OF AN OLD CLERIC

Black chalk on yellow-brown paper.

255 x 190 mm.

c.1522/24.

Stockholm, National Museum.

The signature of Duerer added in the upper left corner.

Later inscription in the lower left corner: *Albert Durer*.

Portrait of an old cleric; the cap with button on top was the type worn by canons. Of the several suggestions made to identify the likeness, the most attractive is that of Zuelch (p. 406), who proposed Johannes de Indagine, comparing the drawing with the portrait of Indagine by Hans Baldung Grien which appears as a woodcut on the title page of his book on physiognomy, 1522 (see No. 35). I acknowledge some similarity, but the difference of age—the drawing shows a much older man—is too great to justify this identification. Neither is the similarity of the drawing to the head of Johannes Pals, the provost of the Neue Stiftskirche at Halle, who stands behind St. Erasmus in the Munich painting (Burkhard, pl. 64), sufficient to allow an identification. But there is a definite similarity in the manner in which the modelling in the drawing is worked out by the most refined painterly means, justifying our dating it definitely at the time when the painting was done, i.e., in 1522-1524. The raised position of the head and the direction of the eyes suggest a study for the figure of a kneeling donor.

Lit.: facsimile: Ges. f. Z. K.; Friedlaender, No. 33; Zuelch, No. 34; Burkhard, No. 29; E. Buchner, Bildnisse der Grafen Thomas und Heinrich von Rineck, in *Wallraf-Richartz Jahrbuch*, 1937.

Copies after Gruenewald Drawings

A3

CHRIST ON THE CROSS

Black chalk, heightened by white; on blue paper.

550 x 340 mm.

Basle, Oeffentliche Kunstsammlung.

Copy of No. 2, probably done by tracing. Since the copy was made before the figure and cross of the original drawing were cut out, it can be used to reconstruct the original contour. Below, the cross is set in a horizontal beam not shown or not preserved in the original. Zuelch raises the question of whether this addition indicates a study for a group in sculpture, but what can be seen is insufficiently clear to support this conjecture.

Lit.: facsimile: Schmid, pl. 39, 40; Schmid, p. 257; Zuelch, No. 2a.

A4

CHRIST ON THE CROSS

Brush, wash and white, producing the effect of gouache; on yellow paper; cut out along the outlines of the cross and body and pasted on different paper.

520 x 410 mm.

17th century.

Basle, Oeffentliche Kunstsammlung.

Copy after an original study by Gruenewald, now lost, for the Christ of the *Isenheim Crucifixion,* its technique suggesting a date in the 17th century. The original was an important link between the *Small* (fig. A6) and the *Isenheim Crucifixion* (fig. A7). Certain features of this drawing are so near to the *Isenheim Crucifixion,* e.g., the body of Christ, the loincloth, that its original can justly be considered to have been a study for that work. The critics who consider it a copy after the *Isenheim Altar* overlook features connecting it with the earlier *Small Crucifixion,* which place it rather, between the two. In the *Isenheim Crucifixion* the inscription IRNI is above the horizontal cross-beam and written in Gothic minuscule; in the drawing it appears beneath the beam in the same place as in the *Small Crucifixion,* and in the same narrow capitals. The fingers are still not so widespread as in the *Isenheim Crucifixion* but placed like those in the *Small Crucifixion.*

Lit.: Schmid, pp. 257-258; Schoenberger, *Staedeljahrbuch* II, 1923; Zuelch, No. 26.

A15

COPY OF THE SELF-PORTRAIT WITH DRAWING-QUILL

Pen over black chalk on yellow-brown paper.

311 x 200 mm.

Early 17th century.

Copy of the signature: M

Inscribed: *Contrafactur des hochberuempten Malers Mathes von Aschaffenburg.*

Kassel, Gemaeldegalerie.

In spite of slight changes, e.g., in the costume, the Kassel copy of Gruenewald's *Self-portrait* furnishes, by its inscription, important evidence for the identification and validity of the Erlangen original (No. 9). By the character of the script the drawing can be dated c.1600, that is, certainly prior to Sandrart's use of the original. (See note to No. 9.) It proves the authenticity of the signature on the original (No. 9); it proves also that the date *1529*, which is not on the copy, is a later addition which apparently was not on the Erlangen drawing when the copy was made. On the reverse side is an inscription by a later hand: *Matheus Gruenewald von Aschaffenburg sehr wahres Portraet von ihm selbst gezeichnet um das Jahr 1500.* This identifies for the first time the drawing in Erlangen as a self-portrait.

Lit.: Schmid, p. 267, pl. 27; Zuelch, No. 14a.

Drawings doubtfully or erroneously attributed to Gruenewald or to his followers

DRAWINGS PUBLISHED BY HANS H. NAUMANN IN LE PREMIER ELEVE DE MARTIN SCHONGAUER IN *ARCHIVES ALSACIENNES*, 1935

Naumann ascribed a great number of drawings dating c.1470-1500 to the young Mathis Gothart Nithart, whom he considers to be a pupil of Schongauer, and whom he identifies with the Hausbuchmeister as well as with the Master of the Bergmann Print-shop. It must be admitted that no one knows the drawing style of Gruenewald before c.1500. But none of the drawings ascribed by Naumann can be proved to be by Gruenewald. It clearly appears that Naumann puts drawings of very different character under one name. There are only three drawings which, by the grandeur of their style of drapery recall later figures of Gruenewald, although they are themselves in the late Gothic angular style: fig. 123, p. 138, Study of Angels, and fig. 124, p. 139, Study of St. John beneath the Cross, both pen drawings (Dijon, Museum). Related to some extent is the Drapery Study, fig. 130, p. 151 (Berlin, Kupferstich-Kabinett). However, the complete lack of works definitely by Gruenewald before 1500 prevents for the time being any undocumented attribution of drawings to this period.

ST. KILIAN

Brown ink on paper.

316 x 187 mm.

Basle, Tobias Christ Collection.

Published by F. Winkler as the work of Hans von Kulmbach (*Old Master Drawings VIII*, 1933-1934), but more recently by Engelbert Baumeister as possibly by Gruenewald (Eine Zeichnung Gruenewalds in *Pantheon XXVI*, 1940). This last is a serious attempt to break into the unknown territory of the early drawings of the master. Baumeister assumes a date c.1500, i.e., before the earliest known works of 1503. There are in fact some formal details which we find similar to those in later works, for example, the hands, but Baumeister does not succeed in widening these observations on detail into a general characterization of Gruenewald's manner. The expression of the face is too distinct and too strongly fixed. The quality of the drawing as a whole is not high enough, and is somewhat overrated by Baumeister. The composition of the right side (the bishop's left) is rather tiresome. We would find already in the early drawings of Gruenewald a more varied and more magnificent general effect. Besides, the drawing has no connection with the School of the Master of the House-book, which we could justifiedly expect to find in early Gruenewald drawings.

HEAD OF A TORTURER FROM A PASSION SCENE

Black chalk and sanguine on paper, turned yellow-brown.

220 x 161 mm.

Paris, Louvre.

Published by Schmid (p. 271) as "vermutlich Gruenewald." Facsimile: Ges. f. Z. K. Schmid emphasizes that its quality is not so high as that of other Gruenewald drawings. The drawing must be eliminated from Gruenewald's oeuvre. The modelling of the exterior and interior forms is much too detailed and sharp. Weinberger suggests that the drawing belongs to the School of the Danube.

HEAD OF AN ANGEL

Grey chalk on yellow paper.

Basle, Oeffentliche Kunstsammlung.

Published by Schmid (p. 272) and by Zuelch (fig. 179, No. 11a) as a copy of a study of an Angel of the Annunciation. The drawing was previously attributed by G. von Therey to Baldung Grien (*Die Handzeichnungen des Hans Baldung Grien* 1, 14); first given to Gruenewald by Rieffel. The almost ornamental way in which the hairs are drawn is far from Gruenewald's manner, but surely indicates the neighborhood of Baldung.

SUSANNA AND THE TWO ELDERS

Black chalk on paper.

92 x 131 mm.

Formerly Haarlem, Koenigs Collection. From Savigny Collection.

First attributed tentatively to Gruenewald by E. Schilling. This is mentioned as a possibility by E. Bock also (*Old Master Drawings* II, 1927, p. 13). Acknowledged by Zuelch and published as No. 1 of his catalogue of the drawings. But the drawing of the nudes differs greatly from all the established drawings of the Master. It has neither the sweeping manner of the Man Blowing a Trumpet (No. 1) or St. Sebastian (Nos. 6-7), nor the detailed finesse of modelling as in the Christ on the Cross (No. 2). It is done with very small strokes, and is rather weak and indistinct. The types, also, have nothing to do with those of Gruenewald. The face of the woman is much too regular to be considered as being by him.

HEAD OF AN OLD WOMAN

Charcoal, heightened with white, on red ground.

260 x 188 mm.

London, British Museum.

Attributed to Gruenewald by Bayersdorfer. Published as Gruenewald in *Vasari Society* II, 29; rejected by Schmid (p. 283), who suggests that it is nearer to Duerer or to Hans v. Kulmbach. The detail forms, as the eyes, nose and mouth are modelled much too distinctly and clearly with draughtsmanlike means to justify the authorship of Gruenewald.

DRAWING OF THE PUMP OF THE MARKET-FOUNTAIN AT HALLE

Pen on paper.

Halle, City Archive Act XV, O 1.

Published by Rolf Huenecken (Gruenewald in Halle, in *Zeitschrift fuer Kunstgeschichte* Vol. V, 1936, p. 238, fig. 9). The attribution is due to the fact that Gruenewald was called to Halle in 1528 as "wasserkunstmacher," i.e., as an expert in fountain construction. Only this drawing is preserved from that time. Huenecken states that the drawing perhaps may be by the hand of Gruenewald himself. But unfortunately there is not the slightest possibility of confirming this tentative attribution. The drawing itself has no specific artistic quality.

ST. ANTHONY VISITING ST. PAUL

By Philipp Uffenbach.

Watercolor on paper.

1590.

Signed and dated in the upper left-hand corner.

Goettingen, Collection of the University.

Published first by Donner von Richter (Philipp Uffenbach, in *Archiv fuer Frankfurts Geschichte und Kunst* III. Folge 7, 1901. See also Zuelch, *Jahresberichte der Oeffentlichen Kunstsammlung*, Basle, Neue Folge vol. 24, 1927, and *Gruenewald*, p. 339). Zuelch considers the drawing as a copy of an original by Gruenewald for the Isenheim Altar-piece. This cannot be. Even if one would consider a drawing by Gruenewald as model its date must be earlier, i.e., at the end of the 15th century, since the drawing belongs still to the late Gothic angular style. But the type of the saint, which is much nearer to Duerer than to Gruenewald (compare woodcut, B. 107), prevents me from agreeing that it is a copy after Gruenewald. Uffenbach displays many influences, not of Gruenewald alone but of Duerer as well.

HEAD OF A MAN FACING TO THE LEFT

Black chalk, heightened with white, on paper.

253 x 209 mm.

From the Savigny Collection.

Published by Elfried Bock in *Old Master Drawings* II, 1927, as by a "follower of Matthias Gruenewald." This drawing surely should not be considered as going back to a Gruenewald original in any respect. The profile is much too sharply formed and the expression too sentimental. The general type is very different from that of Gruenewald. Weinberger suggests the school of Georg Pencz.

NOTES

1 In his notes on the Grimmer family of painters Sandrart mentions Adam and Johannes, or Hans, but in referring to Grimmer as a pupil of Gruenewald he does not give a first name. According to Zuelch (p. 398) both lived in Mainz. Adam Grimmer was the teacher of Philipp Uffenbach, and, considering his dates and those of his father, Hans, only the latter could have been Gruenewald's pupil. But no work is known which would justify this assumption. There is not one work in existence which can be attributed with certainty to Hans Grimmer and every known work of Adam is completely untouched by any tradition of Gruenewald's art. This would not be so if the father's work had been representative of Gruenewald's school. If Sandrart's statement were true, the only conclusion to be drawn from it would be the dubious one that Hans Grimmer did not follow his master at all. Dismissal of Sandrart's theory in this connection does not mean that the drawings of Gruenewald may not have come into Uffenbach's possession in the manner he describes. Uffenbach, as a master of the early Baroque, may well have recognized Gruenewald's importance more clearly than any of the latter's manneristic sixteenth-century followers. What became of the Gruenewald drawings after Abraham Schelkens' death in 1684 is not known. Zuelch suggests (Die ersten Gruenewald Sammler in *Der Kunstwanderer,* 1925-1926) that Schelkens' son Sebastian inherited the treasure. Sebastian Schelkens, a professor who lived in Franecker, Holland, was the owner of a famous collection, which his son-in-law, Professor Lemonon of Franecker, inherited when the former died in 1700. There is, however, no record of this collection's having contained the Gruenewald drawings.

2 The first to connect, even tentatively, the name Mathis Gothart Nithart with the monogram MGN was Oskar Hagen, in a note in the first edition of his book on Gruenewald, in which he discussed Zuelch's article: Gruenewald oder Gruen in *Repertorium fuer Kunstwissenschaft,* XL, 1917, wherein Zuelch had published, also for the first time, documents on a Master Mathis Gothart Nithart. Zuelch answered with an article: Das Dunkel um Gruenewald in *Repertorium fuer Kunstwissenschaft,* XLIII, 1921, publishing the inventory of Mathis Gothart Nithart's possessions, in which he is called "Maler und Wasserkunstmacher," which title prevented Zuelch at that time from agreeing to an identification with Gruenewald. Hagen also, upon acquaintance with the new sources, no longer believed in the possibility of Mathis Gothart Nithart and Gruenewald being the same man, and dropped reference to it in the subsequent editions of his book. The thesis that Mathis Gothart Nithart was Sandrart's Gruenewald, court painter to the Archbishop of Mainz, and the painter of several altar-pieces for the Mainz Cathedral, was proven more conclusively by the find of Grete Thiemann in the Archives of Wuerzburg (published in *Cicerone,* XVI, 1924): the document of a salary payment made in 1516 to "Mathias Gothart pictor" in the court service at Mainz (Source 6). The final proof was afforded when Zuelch found in the Archives of Frankfurt extensive notes on a lawsuit which established the identification of the painter, the engineer and the architect Mathis Gothart Nithart as Gruenewald beyond any doubt. (Eine Gruenewald Urkunde in *Jahresbericht der Oeffentlichen Kunstsammlung, Basel, Neue Folge,* XXIV, 1927.) All these sources are published now in their entirety in Zuelch's book: *Der Historische Gruenewald,* 1938.

3 On the panel showing the St. Lawrence of the Heller Altar, now Frankfurt, Staedelsches Kunstinstitut (Burkhard, pl. 8) and on the frame of the Aschaffenburg Altar (fig. A24).

4 Heinz Braune's assumption (*Muenchner Jahrbuch* N.F. IV, 1927) that the painting is a copy, made by Gruenewald between 1500 and 1510, after an earlier model, is wrong. The painting is an original of c.1480, probably a posthumous portrait since the Pfalzgraf Friedrich represented died in 1477.

5 See E. Panofsky, *Albrecht Duerer*, I, p. 146f.

6 Edgar Wind in his Studies in Allegorical Portraiture in *Journal of the Warburg Institute*, I, 1937-1938, tries to establish a date between 1516-1518 for the St. Erasmus panel. As much as I agree with Wind's iconographical interpretation of the painting, I think we must stick to a date between 1520 and 1523, which is usually given to that painting. It is a fact, not taken seriously enough into consideration by Wind, that the huge silver reliquary of St. Maurice at the Neue Stiftskirche at Halle is not included in the printed *Heiltumsbuch* of Halle of 1520. Since this reliquary is the most important iconographical source for the figure of St. Maurice in Gruenewald's painting, and since, if it had been part of the church treasure in 1520, it would certainly have been listed in the *Heiltumsbuch*, this date is a clear terminus post for the painting. The fact that Albrecht's coat of arms on the painting does not show the cardinal's hat which he had acquired in 1518 is sufficiently explained by Albrecht's appearance in the figure of St. Erasmus: it would have been very immodest to put his rank above the one of the Saint. There is another representation of Albrecht as St. Martin (Eltville, Siersdorpf Collection), surely painted after 1520, with Albrecht's coat of arms, again without the cardinal's hat.

7 See Note 1.

8 August Feigel, Skulpturen im Stil Gruenewalds in *Muenchner Jahrbuch,* II, 1909. Adolf Fuelner, Ein Zinnkruzifix nach Gruenewald in *Staedeljahrbuch*, VIII, 1932; Alfred Wolters, Eine Gruenewaldreminiszenz in *Staedeljahrbuch,* II, 1922; Alfred Neumeyer, Gruenewalds Gewandstil in *Festschrift fuer Adolf Goldschmidt,* 1935.

9 Sandrart's note about woodcuts of an Apocalypse (see Source 17) is very vague. He surely did not see the prints himself. Yet this note produced, in one of the worst books on Gruenewald, by Friedrich Knapp (Bielefeld und Leipzig, 1935), the senseless pretention that some of the woodcuts of Duerer's Apocalypse were actually by Gruenewald. It is sometimes assumed that a cycle of Apocalypse woodcuts by Matthias Gerung misled Sandrart, owing to a similar *MG* monogram.

10 See Sources 14, 16 and Catalogue notes 6, 7.

11 See Catalogue note 35.

12 The color of the paper differs considerably from very light to deep yellow-brown.

13 Apparent especially in the works of Cranach and Hans Baldung Grien.

14 See Catalogue notes 19, 31, 32.

15 See Catalogue notes 34, 35.

16 See H. A. Schmid, *Gemaelde und Zeichnungen von Matthias Gruenewald,* Page 291: Melanchthon, *Elementorum rethorices libri duo.* 1531 (last chapter).

17 See E. Panofsky, *Albrecht Duerer,* Vol. II, fig. 140.

18 See E. Panofsky, *Albrecht Duerer,* Vol. II, fig. 199 and Vol. I, p. 147.

19 Unfortunately I have not been able to obtain a copy of this article.

SOURCES

1

1511-1512   Lawsuit of Conrad Ulner against Hans Martinstein, Frankfurt-on-Main, Archives of the City, mentioning Gruenewald's work in the Dominican monastery at Frankfurt

Als Mayster Mathys nach folgens hie [i.e., in Frankfurt] zu den predigern eyn tafel gemoelet hat ist Conrad Ulner ins Closter gegangen und hat Mathysen umb seinen verdientten lidlon arrestieren und bekommeren wollen one das Conratten solichs zu thun vergundt worden, und das ist war.

2

1514   Last Will of Canon Heinrich Reitzmann, Wuerzburg, State Archives

Donation of the Altar of the Virgin of the Snows of Aschaffenburg and the Altar of Oberissigheim

Item similiter volo et ordino quod festum Nivis gloriossissime Marie virginis in tabula depingatur prout in proximo elapso anno in testamento meo ordinavi. [The will of 1513 is missing.]

Item decimatores in Uskem tenentur mihi de Annis 1510, 1511, 1513, prout in registris meis continetur, et in presente anno 1514 decima ipsis locata est pro LX fl. de quibus debitis lego ad fabricam ibidem in Uskem XXX florenos, ut ibidem fiat nova tabula cum quatuor ymaginibus in summo altare, videlicet gloriossissime Marie virginis in medio, Sanctorum Vincentii patroni in dextro, Hieronimi in sinistro et sancti Georgii patroni in pede tabule equitando etc prout magistro Matheo in selgenstat optime constat, qui locum me presente vidit, et reliquum debitum dividetur equaliter. . . .

3

c.1515-1516   Inscription around the arch of the lunette of the Altar in the Chapel of the Virgin of the Snows, Aschaffenburg, Collegiate Church

MARIA MATER GRACIE MATER MISERICORDIAE TU NOS AB HOSTE PROTEGE

4

c.1515-1516   Inscription in the lunette of the frame of the Altar in the Chapel of the Virgin of the Snows, Aschaffenburg, Collegiate Church

AD DIVAM MARIAM VIRGINEM DE NIVE. ASPICE MORTALES PLACIDIS PIA MATER OCULIS EXCRUCIANT VARIIS QUOS SUA FATA MODIS

5

1516   Dedication of the Chapel of the Virgin of the Snows in Aschaffenburg, Collegiate Church. Coat of arms of Albrecht of Mainz: . . . SACELLUM HOC ET ALTARE CONSECRAVIT ET INDULGENTIIS DOTAVIT 1516 KALENDIS NOVEMBRIS

6

1516   Salary payment for *Mathis maler*, Wuerzburg, State Archives, Proceedings of the Chapter of Mainz Cathedral

Lecta fuit supplicatio magistri Mathie Gothart pictoris, quibus petit reverendissimi domini locum tenentes induci, ut computo facto ipso de salario suo contentent atque satisfatiant. Super

quo commissum fuit domino Johanni de Guttenberg, ut dominum de Koenigstein accedat et nomine capituli roget ut sibi satisfiat.

7

1517   Last Will of Canon Heinrich Reitzmann, Wuerzburg, State Archives

Item lego XXV florenos ad faciendum pingere festum Niuis per magistrum matheum pinctorem in tabulam iam confectam, que locari debet in nova capella dominorum Casparis et Georgii Schantzen fratrum, materialia, utpote colores, reperiuntur in mensa serata in aula.

8

1519   Inscription on the socle of the Altar of the Chapel of the Virgin of the Snows in Aschaffenburg, Collegiate Church

AD HONOREM FESTI NIVIS DEI PAERAE VIRGINIS HENRICHUS RETZMAN HUIUS AEDIS CUSTOS ET CANONICUS AC GASPAR SCHANTZ CANONICUS EIUSDEM E. C. 1519 MGN

9

1522 (1543)   Johannes de Indagine, Introductiones . . . in chiromantiam, phisiognomiam, etc. Paris, 1543

Pars I: Physiognomia ex aspectu membrorum hominis

p. 47 r.: *De iudicio oculorum . . . Quibus [oculi] in morem vitellorum propendent extra foramine . . . crassum et hebetem, et ad hoc etiam luxuriosum, pigrum, mendacem, simplicum significant . . . Siquibus compressi sunt et velut ad scopum intentibus crudeles tyrannos. Ubi vero deflaccescunt voluunturque ultro citroque . . . impudicos arrogantes instabiles mendaces [significant].*

p. 49 r.: *De oris physiognomia . . . Os aut magnum est et patulum aut augustum . . . augustum: retentorem arcanorum, modestum sobrium, pudicum, timidem. Patens: audacem, obstreperum, impudicum, mendacem, impostorem, luxuriosum [significat].*

p. 50: *Nasus recurrus sive aduncus vel preacutus semper iram audaciam tyranidem notat.*

p. 56r.: *. . . Glabra et complanata cuticula nisi intra supernam superficiam nasi prophanum fallacem iracundum significat.*

10

1527   Drawing of a water-mill for the City of Magdeburg

Frankfurt-on-Main, Archives of the City, Buergermeisterbuch, 1527, folio 19

Maister Mathissen dem Maler der muhlen Contravision zu machen begunstigen wie der [Rat?] von Maydburg [i.e., Magdeburg] begert hat.

11

1527   Birthplace of Gruenewald

From a lawsuit of Gruenewald against Hans Ruckus, a tailor

Frankfurt-on-Main, Archives of the City

Meister Mathis von Wuertzburg maler spricht zu Hans Ruckus schnider vor 4 gulden gelihenes gelt . . .

12

1528   Gruenewald's death

Frankfurt-on-Main, City Archives, Buergermeisterbuch, 1528, September 10

Als Ratman, meyster der Innungen und gemeynheit der stat Hall (i.e., Halle) schriben meister

Mathes Gothart maler oder wasserkunstmacher, der ein testament gemacht und hinder Hans sy-
densticker zum Einhorn ligen sol . . . nach Hans sydenstickern schicken das testament herfur-
zuthun.

13

1528   Inventory of the estate of Gruenewald (Excerpt)

                 Meister Mathis maler

Anno domini 1528 uff mitwoch nach Galli haben wir Jo[han] F[ichart], Johan Bischoff als
weltlicher richter und Hans Felser richter als zugen inventirt die narung meister Mathis maler
[maler crossed out*] Nithart ader Gothart nach im hinder Meister Hansen sydenstick[ern] von*
Sarbrucken gehabt, inventirt als folget:

item. 1 cleyn buchelgin ingebunden, erclerung der 12 artikeln des christlichen glaubens

item. 27 predeg Lutters ingebunden

item. 1 versigelt vertragsbrieff zwischen meister Mathissen und meister Micheln von Altkirch
1513 [i.e., Altkirch in Alsace, near Isenheim]

item. 1 vertrag zwischen ime und Michel Wesser 1515

item. 6 gebuelten [?] mit formen angesicht [drawing of heads?]

item. das nu testament ingebunden und sunst viel schartecken luterich

14

1570-1586   Inventories of Basilius Amerbach, Basle

             Basle, Oeffentliche Kunstsammlung (Schmid, p. 294)

             Inventory A, in a group of prints and drawings: *Aschenburg* (i.e., Mathis von Aschaff-
enburg) *10*

             Inventory B, in the third drawer a folder with drawings by Hans Leu and: *Math[is]*
Aschenburg

             Inventory C, in a cupboard with drawings: *Mathis Aschenburg 20*

15

1664   Journal des Voyages de Monsieur de Monconys, Lyon 1665-1666. Seconde Partie. Voy-
age d'Angleterre, Paies-Bas, Allemagne & Italie. p. 280

Le 5 [Janvier] L'Apresdiné M. Marcel peintre & frère de nostre hoste me mena chez M. Chele-
kens qui a des tableaux & de très beaux livres d'Estamps, entre autres un de toutes les oeuvres de
Israel Van Mocre [i.e., Israel van Meckenem] *plus ancien qu' Albert* [i.e., Duerer]. *Un de*
toutes les oeuvres d'Albert en cuivre, & un autre de toutes celles de bois, entre lesquelles est ca belle
porte triomphale, & un autre livre des desseins d'un Martin [i.e., Mathis] *d'Achafenbourg, bien*
plus estimé infiniment qu'Albert Dure, mais peu connu en France.

16

1668   Catalogue of the Art Collection of B. L. Kuenast, Strassbourg

Kunstbuecher von Kupferstichen, Contrefaict getuscht und gerissene Sachen:

A   *ein Buch in Grossfolio 1920 Stueck*

B   *ein anderes dito 723 Stueck von Urs Graf, Hieronimus Cock, Matheus Grien* [Gruene-
wald], *Wolf Huber, etc.*

1675

Joachim von Sandrart, "Teutsche Academie der Edlen Bau-, Bild-, und Mahlerey-Kuenste.". . . Nuremberg 1675

[on the margin:]
Matthaeus
Gruenewald
von Aschen-
burg/Mahler

II Teil, 3, (p. 236)

Matthaeus Gruenewald, sonst Matthaeus von Aschaffenburg genant, doerf unter allen den baes-ten Geistern der alten Teutschen in der edlen Zeichen- und Mahl-Kunst keinem weichen oder etwas nachgeben, sondern er ist in der Warheit den fuertreflichsten und baesten wo nicht mehrer doch gleich zu schaetzen. Es ist aber zu bedauren, dass dieser ausbuendige Mann dermassen mit seinen Werken in Vergessenheit gerahten, dass ich nicht einen Menschen mehr bey Leben weiss, der von seinem Thun nur eine geringe Schrift oder muendliche Nachricht geben koente; Damit jedoch seine Wuerdigkeit an Tag gebracht werde, will ich mit besonderm Fleiss, soviel mir bewust, anziehen, ohne welches ich glaube, dass dieses schoene Gedaechtnis in wenig Jahren ganz voellig erloeschen wuerde. Es sind bereits 50 Jahr verflossen, dass ein sehr alter aber kunstreicher Mahler zu Frank-furt Namens Philipp Uffenbach gelebet, der vormals ein Lehrjung des beruehmten Teutschen Mahlers Grimers gewesen; dieser Grimer hat bey ermeldtem Matthaeus von Aschaffenburg gel-ernet und alles, was er von ihme koennen zusammen tragen, fleissig aufgehoben; absonderlich hat

*Seine
Handrisse*

er nach seines Lehrmeisters Tod von desselben Wittib allerhand herrliche Handrisse, meistens mit schwarzer Kreid und theils fast Lebens-Groesse gezeichnet, bekommen, welche alle nach dieses Grimers Ableiben obgedachter Philipp Uffenbach als ein nachsinnlicher beruehmter Mann an sich gebracht; damals gienge ich unweit seiner Behausung zu Frankfurt in die Schul und wartete ihme offtmals auf, da er mir dann, wann er in gutem humor ware, diese in ein Buch zusammen gesamlete edle Handrisse des Matthaeus von Aschaffenburg, als dessen Art er fleissig nachstudirte, gezeigt und derselben loebliche Qualitaeten und Wolstand entdecket. Dieses ganze Buch ist nach gedachten Uffenbachs Tod von seiner Wittfrauen dem beruehmten Kunstlieber, Herrn Abra-ham Schelkens zu Frankfurt theur verkauft und von demselben neben vielen anderen herrlichen Kunststuecken von den baesten alten und modernen Gemaehlden raren Buechern und Kupfer-stichen, die viel zu lang zu erzehlen fallen wuerden, in sein beruehmt Kunst-Cabinet zu ewiger

Gedaechtnis

Gedaechtnis dieser ruhmwuerdigen Hand und allen Kunstliebenden suesser Vergnuegung gestel-let worden, wohin ich also den guenstigen Leser will gewiesen haben.

*Seine Werke
zu Frankfurt*

Dieser fuertrefliche Kuenstler hat zur Zeit Albert Duerers ungefehr Anno 1505 gelebet, welches an dem Altar von der Himmelfahrt Mariae in der Prediger Closter zu Frankfurt von Albrecht Duerer gefaertiget abzunehmen, als andessen vier Fluegel von aussenher, wann der Altar zuge-schlossen wird, dieser Matthaeus von Aschaffenburg mit liecht in grau und schwarz diese Bilder gemahlt; auf einem ist S. Lorenz mit dem Rost, auf dem andern eine S. Elisabeth, auf dem dritten S. Stephan und auf dem vierdten ein ander Bild, so mir entfallen, sehr zierlich gestellet, wie es noch allda zu Frankfurt zu sehen. Absonderlich aber ist sehr preiswuerdig die von ihme mit Wasser-farben gebildete Verklaerung Christi auf den Berg Thabor, als worinnen zuvorderst eine ver-wunderlich-schoene Wolke, darinnen Moyses und Elias erscheinen, samt denen auf der Erden knienden Apostlen, von Invention, Colorit und allen Zierlichkeiten so fuertreflich gebildet, dass es Selzamkeit halber von nichts uebertroffen wird, ja es ist in Manier und Eigenschaft unvergleich-lich und eine Mutter aller Gratien.

Zu Maynz

Ferner waren von dieser edlen Hand zu Maynz in dem Domm auf der linken Seiten des Chors in drey unterschiedlichen Capellen drey Altar-Blaetter, jedes mit zweyen Fluegeln in- und auswen-dig gemahlt gewesen, deren erstes war unsere liebe Frau mit dem Christkindlein in der Wolken unten zur Erden warten viele Heiligen in sonderbarer Zierlichkeit auf, als S. Catharina, Bar-bara, Caecilia, Elisabetha, Apollonia und Ursula, alle dermassen adelich, natuerlich, holdselig und correct gezeichnet, auch so wol colorirt, dass sie mehr im Himmel als auf Erden zu seyn schie-nen. Auf ein anderes Blat war gebildet ein blinder Einsidler, der mit seinem Leitbuben ueber den zugefrornen Rheinstrom gehend auf dem Eiss von zween Moerdern ueberfallen und zu todt geschlagen wird und auf seinem schreynden Knaben ligt, an Affecten und Ausbildung mit verwunderlich natuerlichen wahren Gedanken gleichsam ueberhaeuft anzusehen; das dritte Blat war etwas inperfecter als vorige zwey und sind sie zusammen Anno 1631 oder 32 in damaligem wilden Krieg weggenommen und in einem Schiff nach Schweden versandt worden, aber neben vielen andern dergleichen Kunststuecken durch Schiffbruch in dem Meer zu Grund gegangen.

Zu Eysenach [i.e. Isenheim]

Es soll auch noch ein Altar-Blat in Eysenach von dieser Hand seyn und darinnen ein verwunderlicher S. Antonio, worinnen die Gespenster hinter den Fenstern gar artig ausgebildet seyn sollen; Ferner haben Ihre Fuerstl. Durchl. Herzog Wilhelm in Bayern hochseligsten Andenkens als vernuenftiger Urtheiler und Liebhaber der edlen Kunst ein klein Crucifix mit unser lieben Frauen und S. Johann samt einer niderknienden und andaechtigbetenden Maria Magdalena so fleissig gemahlt von dieser Hand gehabt, auch sehr geliebt, ohne dass sie gewust, von wem es sey.

Ein sehr natuerlich Crucifix.

Selbiges ist wegen des verwunderlichen Christus am Creutz, so ganz abhenkend auf den Fuessen ruhet, sehr seltsam, dass es das wahre Leben nicht anderst thun koente; und gewiss ueber alle Crucifix natuerlich wahr und eigentlich ist, wann ihm mit vernuenftiger Gedult lang nachgesonnen wird. Solches ist deswegen halb-Bogen gross auf gnaedigen Befehl hochgedachten Herzogs Anno 1605 von Raphael Sadler in Kupfer gestochen worden, und erfreute sich hernachmalen Ihre Churfuerstl. Durchl. Maximilian seligster Gedaechtnis hoechlich, da ich des Meisters Namen geoffenbaret.

Wiederum gehet in Holzshnitt aus die Offenbarung des heiligen Johannes, ist aber uebel zu bekommen und solle auch von dieser Hand seyn; gleichfals ist zu meiner Zeit in Rom ein heiliger Johannes mit zusammengeschlagnen Haenden, das Angesicht ueber sich, ob er Christum am Creutz anschauete, gewesen, ueberaus andaechtig und beweglich in Lebens-Groesse mit herrlicher gratia, so aestimirt und auch hoch fuer Albert Duerers Arbeit geschaezt worden; da ich aber, von wem es waere erkandt, und den Unterschied der Manier gezeigt, habe ich gleich hintenher mit Oelfarbe (womit ich eben damals des Papsts Contrafaet machte) dessen Namen also setzen muessen: Matthaeus Gruenwald Alemann fecit. Und das ist es nun, was von dieses fuertreflichen Teutschen Kunst-Stucken mir bewust, ausser dass er sich meistens zu Maynz aufgehalten und ein eingezogenes melancholisches Leben gefuehrt und uebel verheuratet gewesen; wo und wann er gestorben, ist mir unbekandt, halte doch darfuer dass es um An. 1510. geschehen. Sein Contrafaet zeiget die Kupferblatte CC.

18

1679
Sandrart, op. cited, III. 3, p. 68

[on margin] Mathaeus Gruenwald von Aschaffenburg

Von diesem vortrefflichen hochgestiegenen Geist und verwunderlichen Meister haben wir in unserem vorigen Buch am 236. Blat, seiner uberfliegenden Erfahrenheit zum Nachruhm, weitlaeufftige Meldungen gethan; Was er nemlich fuer herrliche Wercke zu Franckfurt bey den Prediger Muenchen gemacht: als zum Exempel auf ein Altarblat die seelige Elisabeth, S. Stephan, S. Lorentz und R. oberhalb dessen auch die Verklaerung unsers seligmachers Jesu Christi auf dem Berge Thabor, da Ihme Moses und Elias in den Wolcken erschienen, imgleichen auch unten an dem Berge die in Furcht gantz verzuckte Apostel, wie nicht weniger die zu Mayntz im Thum

Bey Herrn Resident Spiering etliche Tafeln Bey Herrn Schelkens zu Franckfurt ist sein gantz Studium, alles beysammen zu sehen

gestandene, von den Schweden aber hinweg genommene Altaere; und was sonst von ihme der beruehmte Vatter aller Kuenste, Herr Peter Spiring von Nordtholm in Gravenhaag, in seinen beruehmten Haenden gehabt. Massen hiervon bey Herrn Abraham Schelkens zu Frankfurt die meiste von seiner eigenen Hand aufs allervollkommenste gezeichnete Modelle annoch zu ersehen geben, was dieser fuer ein ungemeiner Meister gewest, bey dem Natur und Geist Wunder gethan. Ich meines Theils habe so viel hiervon Bericht gethan, als ich erfahren koennen und auch dem vorigen Teil sein Contrafait mit eingefuegt, welches Albrecht Duerer nach ihme damals, wie sie des Jakob Hellers Altar in obgedachter Prediger-Muench Kirchen zu Frankfurt aufgericht, verfertigt. Wie in der Platte CC. zusehen. Weil aber selbiges nach seiner damaligen Jugend gebildet ist; und seit dem der curioese Hr. Philipp Jacob Stromer, ein Herr der Rathes hiesiger (Nuernberg) hochloebl. Reichsstadt, in seinem bruehmten Kunst-Cabinet, ein noch aelters und perfecters Contrafeyt von gedachtem Meister mir gezeiget: als habe ich billich solches, diesem hochgestiegenen teutschen Coreggio zu Ehren, hie in der Platt. 4. beyfuegen und theilhafftig machen wollen. (No. 9 and figs. A17 and A18)

55

19

1683 Sandrart, op. cited. Latin edition, 1683, p. 225

Sexaginta autem jam anni sunt et quod excurrit, quod pictor . . . . Philippus Uffenbach discipulus quondam Grimeri, cuius Matthaeus hic fuerat praeceptor, mihi enarraret, Grimerum hunc omnia preceptoris sui diagraphica undiquaque collecta sedulo custodivisse et post mortem illius, ab eiusdem vidua potissimum, varia creta nigra et quaedam viventium quantitate delineata accepisse. — — — partesque illorum (diagraphicorum) *optimas, quas sedulo imitabatur, demonstrare solebat.*

BIBLIOGRAPHICAL REFERENCES

General Books and Studies on Gruenewald

BURKHARD, ARTHUR. Matthias Gruenewald, Personality and Accomplishment, Cambridge, Mass., 1936. With bibliography (quoted as: Burkhard)

FEURSTEIN, HEINRICH. Matthias Gruenewald, Bonn, 1930 (quoted as: Feurstein)

FRAENGER, WILHEIM. Matthias Gruenewald, Ein physiognomischer Versuch, Berlin, 1936 (quoted as: Fraenger)

HAGEN, OSKAR. Matthias Gruenewald, Fourth edition, Munich, 1923 (quoted as: Hagen)

HAUSENBERG, MARGARETHE. Matthias Gruenewald im Wandel der deutschen Kunstanschauung, Leipzig, 1927

KAUTZSCH, RUDOLF. Gruenewald, in Bericht ueber die Verhandlungen des Kunsthistorischen Kongresses in Luebeck, 1900

KAYSER, STEPHEN S. Gruenewald's Christianity, in The Review of Religion, 1940

SCHMID, HEINRICH ALFRED. Die Gemaelde und Zeichnungen von Matthias Gruenewald, Vol. 1, plates, Vol. 2, text, Strassburg, 1908 and 1911 (quoted as: Schmid)

ZUELCH, WALTER KARL. Der historische Gruenewald, Mathis Gothardt-Neithardt, Munich, 1938. With sources and bibliography (quoted as: Zuelch)

Publications of Gruenewald's Drawings

FRIEDLAENDER, MAX J. Die Gruenewald Zeichnungen der Sammlung von Savigny, Berlin, 1926 (quoted as: Friedlaender, Savigny Drawings)

FRIEDLAENDER, MAX J. Die Zeichnungen von Matthias Gruenewald, Berlin, 1927 (quoted as: Friedlaender)

GRAUL, RICHARD. Gruenewalds Zeichnungen, Leipzig, 1935 (Inselbuecherei)

GRUENEWALD HANDZEICHNUNGEN, Basle, 1946

STORCK, W. F. Die Handzeichnungen des Matthias Gruenewald, Munich, 1922 (Gesellschaft fuer zeichnende Kuenste). (quoted as: Ges. f. Z. K.)

General Drawing Publications, including Gruenewald

BOCK, ELFRIED. Beschreibendes Verzeichnis saemtlicher Zeichnungen im Kupferstichkabinett zu Berlin, Deutsche Meister. Vols. 1 & 2, Berlin, 1921.

BOCK, ELFRIED. Die Zeichnungen in der Universitaetsbibliothek zu Erlangen, Frankfurt o. M., 1929

COLVIN, SIDNEY. Selected drawings from old masters in the University Galleries and in the library at Christ Church, Oxford, Part II, 1904

DEMONTS, M. Musée du Louvre, Inventaire général des dessins des Ecoles du Nord, I, Paris, 1937

FRIEDLAENDER, MAX J. Zeichnungen alter Meister im Kupferstichkabinett zu Berlin, Berlin, 1920

HAGEN, OSKAR. Deutsche Zeichner von der Gotik bis zum Rokoko, Munich, 1921

KOCH, CARL. Zeichnungen altdeutscher Meister zur Zeit Duerers, Dresden, 1922 (Arnolds Graphische Buecher)

MEDER, JOSEPH. Albertina Facsimile, Vienna, 1920

SAUERMANN, HANS. Deutsche Stilisten, Handzeichnungen alter Meister, Munich, 1914

SCHILLING, EDMUND. Altdeutsche Meisterzeichnungen, Frankfurt o. M., 1934

TIETZE, HANS. European Master Drawings in the United States, New York, 1947

TOLNAY, CHARLES DE. History and Technique of Old Master Drawings, New York, H. Bittner and Co., 1943

WINKLER, FRIEDRICH. Meisterzeichnungen, Vol. IV: Niederrheinische und Westfaelische Handzeichnungen des 15. und 16. Jahrhunderts, Freiburg i. Br., 1932

WINKLER-LIPPMANN. Duerer Zeichnungen, Vol. VI, Berlin, 1927

Special Studies on Gruenewald's Drawings

ANKWICZ VON KLEEHOVEN, H. Zu Gruenewalds Altersportrait, in Graphische Kuenste, New Series, Vol. 3, 1939, No. 3

BAUMEISTER, ENGELBERT. Eine Zeichnung Gruenewalds, in Muenchner Jahrbuch, New Series, Vol. III, 1926

BAUMEISTER, ENGELBERT. Eine Zeichnung Gruenewalds?, in Pantheon 26, 1940

BECKER, FELIX. Zwei neuaufgefundene Gruenewaldzeichnungen (Luetzschena), in Zeitschrift fuer bildende Kunst, New Series, Vol. XXV, 1914

BENESCH, OTTO. The Art of the Renaissance in Northern Europe, Cambridge, 1945

BOCK, ELFRIED. Die aus der Sammlung von Savigny erworbenen Zeichnungen Gruenewalds, in Berichte der Berliner Museen, Vol. XLVI, 1925

BOCK, ELFRIED. Eine Bildniszeichnung Gruenewalds in Weimar, in Jahrbuch der Preussischen Kunstsammlungen, Vol. XLVI, 1925

FRIEDLAENDER, MAX J. Zwei Gruenewald Zeichnungen, in Jahrbuch der Preussischen Kunstsammlungen, Vol. XXXIX, 1918

GANZ, PAUL AND MAJOR, EMIL. Erwaehnung Mathis Aschenburgs in den Amerbachschen Inventaren von 1578, in Jahresbericht LIX (1907) der Oeffentlichen Kunstsammlung zu Basel

GLASER, KURT. Die Gruenewald Zeichnungen der Sammlung von Savigny, in Kunst und Kuenstler, Vol. 24, 1926

HAKEL, A. Die Trinitaet des Boesen, Dissertation, Heidelberg, 1931

HUENECKEN, R. Gruenewald in Halle, in Zeitschrift fuer Kunstgeschichte, Vol. 5, 1936

INDAGINE, JOHANNES DE. Introductiones . . . . in chiromantiam, phisiognomiam, astrologiam naturalem, complexiones hominum, naturas planetarum, Strassburg, Schott, 1522. Second edition, 1534; Paris, Regnault, 1543

KAYSER, STEPHEN. Madonna as Queen of Heaven, in Parnassus, Vol. 11, 1939

KEHRER, HUGO. Zur Deutung einer Gruenewald-Zeichnung im Kupferstichkabinett zu Berlin, in Forschung zur Kirchengeschichte und zur christlichen Kunst (Festgabe zu Joh. Fickers 70. Geburtstag von Freunden und seinen Schuelern), Leipzig, 1931

KEHRER, HUGO. Noch ein Wort zur Deutung einer Gruenewald-Zeichnung (Engel der Verkuendigung), in Muenchner Jahrbuch, New Series, Vol. X, 1933

KOEHN, H. Die Einsiedlertafel des Isenheimer Altars und das Problem des Stifterbildes, in Wallraf-Richartz Jahrbuch, Vol. 2, 1939

KUHLMANN, E. Vrais et faux visages de Gruenewald, in Gazette des Beaux Arts, Series 6, Vol. 20, 1938

LEHRS, MAX. Vier neue Gruenewald Zeichnungen, in Mitteilungen aus den Saechsischen Kunstsammlungen, Vol. I, 1910

MACKERT, E. Trias Romana. Zur Deutung einer Gruenewald Zeichnung, in Westdeutsches Jahrbuch fuer Kunstgeschichte, 1943

MAJOR, EMIL. Das Faeschische Museum und die Faeschichen Inventare, Oeffentliche Kunstsammlung in Basel, 60. Jahresbericht, Neue Folge, Vol. IV, 1908

MEDER, JOSEPH. Eine neue Gruenewald Zeichnung, in Graphische Kuenste, Vol. 43, 1920

MUENZEL, G. Interpretation einer Gruenewald Zeichnung im Kupferstichkabinett zu Berlin, in Berichte der Berliner Museum, Vol. 53, 1932

NAUMANN, HANS H. Mathis Nithart, Le premier élève de Martin Schongauer, in Archives Alsaciennes d'histoire et d'art, 1935, printed separately, Paris, 1936

PARISET, F. G. Autour de Gruenewald, in Gazette des Beaux Arts, Vol. II, 1931

PELTZER, R. A. Joachim von Sandrarts Academie der Bau-Bild und Mahlerey-Kuenste, Munich, 1925

SCHOENBERGER, GUIDO. Gruenewalds Zeichnungen fuer den Isenheimer Altar, in Buchner und Feuchtmayr, Beitraege zur Geschichte der Deutschen Kunst, Vol. I, 1924

SCHOENBERGER, GUIDO. Gruenewalds Klein-Kruzifix, in Staedeljahrbuch, Vol. II, 1922

SCHOENBERGER, GUIDO. Review of Friedlaender, Die Gruenewald Zeichnungen der Sammlung von Savigny, in Oberrheinische Kunst, Vol. I, 1925-1926

SCHRADE, HUBERT. Gruenewalds Selbstbildnis in Erlangen, in Cicerone, Vol. 5, 1923

SCHRADE, HUBERT. Gruenewaldselbstbildnisse, in Zeitschrift fuer Bildende Kunst, Vol. 59, 1925

TIETZE, HANS. The mother of Hans von Schoenitz, in Burlington Magazine, Vol. 44, 1924

WEISBACH, WERNER. Matthias Gruenewald, Formales und Psychologisches, in Kunst und Kuenstler, Vol. 16, 1918

WIND, EDGAR. Charity, in Journal of the Warburg Institute, Vol. I, 1937-1938

WIND, EDGAR. Sante Pagnini and Michelangelo, in Gazette des Beaux Arts Ser. VI, Vol. XXVI, 1947

WINKLER, FRIEDRICH. Duerers Gruenewald Bildnis, in Belvedere (Forum), 1925

ZUELCH, W. K. Ein Beitrag zur Gruenewald Kenntnis und Wertung um 1840, aus dem Nachlass von G. Mueller, in Repertorium fuer Kunstwissenschaft, Vol. 45, 1925

ZUELCH, W. K. Die ersten Gruenewald-Sammler, in Der Kunstwanderer, Vol. 8, 1926

ADDENDA

Recently appeared: R. Pettazzoni, The Pagan Origins of the Three-headed Representation of the Christian Trinity in *Journal of the Warburg and Courtauld Institutes,* Vol. IX, 1946. Pettazzoni states that the three-headed Trinity as well as the three-headed devil are both derived independently from three-headed pagan divinities, the respective representations of the devil being even older than those of the divine Trinity.

Nº 183

1 MAN BLOWING A TRUMPET

2 CHRIST ON THE CROSS

3 WOMAN BENEATH THE CROSS

4 WOMAN BENEATH THE CROSS

5 ST. MAGDALEN BENEATH THE CROSS

6 HANDS AND ARMS OF ST. SEBASTIAN

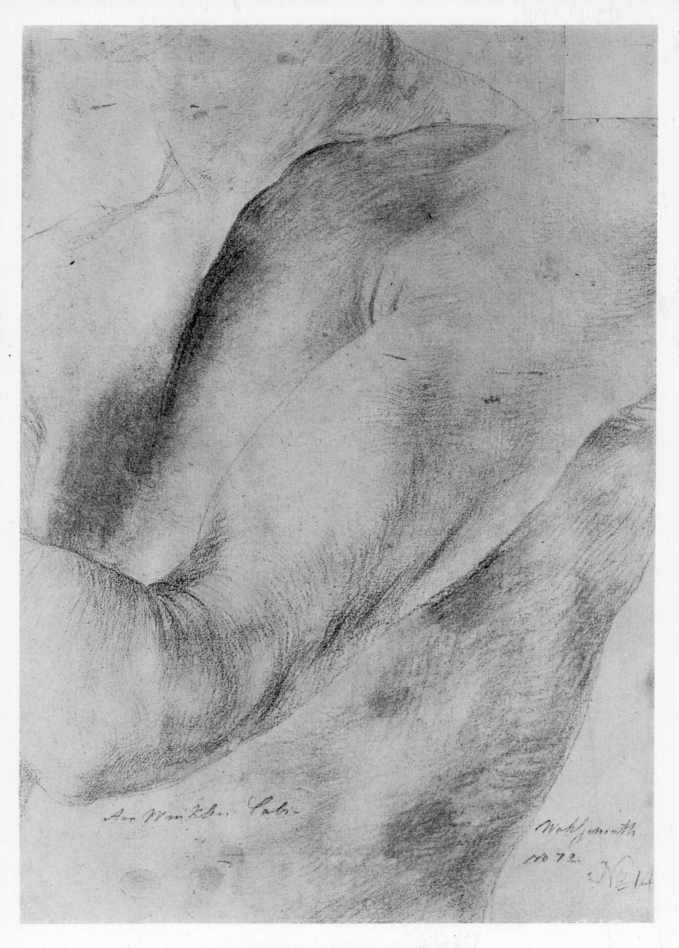

7 UPPER ARMS AND CHEST OF ST. SEBASTIAN

8 PORTRAIT OF GUIDO GUERSI

9 SELF-PORTRAIT OF MASTER MATHIS

10 ST. ANTHONY IN THE DESERT

11 ST. ANTHONY IN THE DESERT

12　THE VIRGIN MARY OF THE ANNUNCIATION

13 GARMENT STUDY FOR THE TRANSFIGURATION

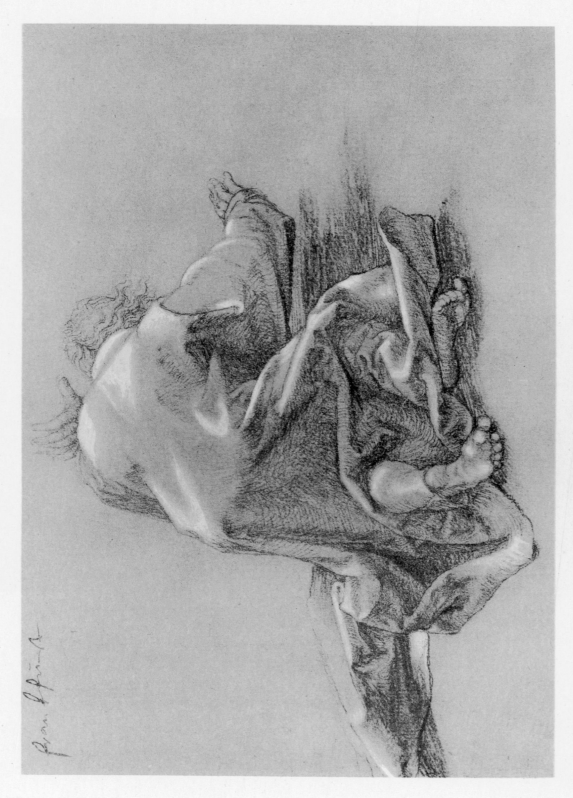

14 APOSTLE OF THE TRANSFIGURATION

15 ST. PETER OF THE TRANSFIGURATION

16 PROPHET OF THE TRANSFIGURATION

17 CHRIST OF A CROWNING OF THE VIRGIN

18 UNFINISHED STUDY FOR ST. PETER

19 SAINT IN LANDSCAPE (ST. PAUL?)

20 VIRGIN AND CHILD WITH ST. JOHN

21 VIRGIN AND CHILD

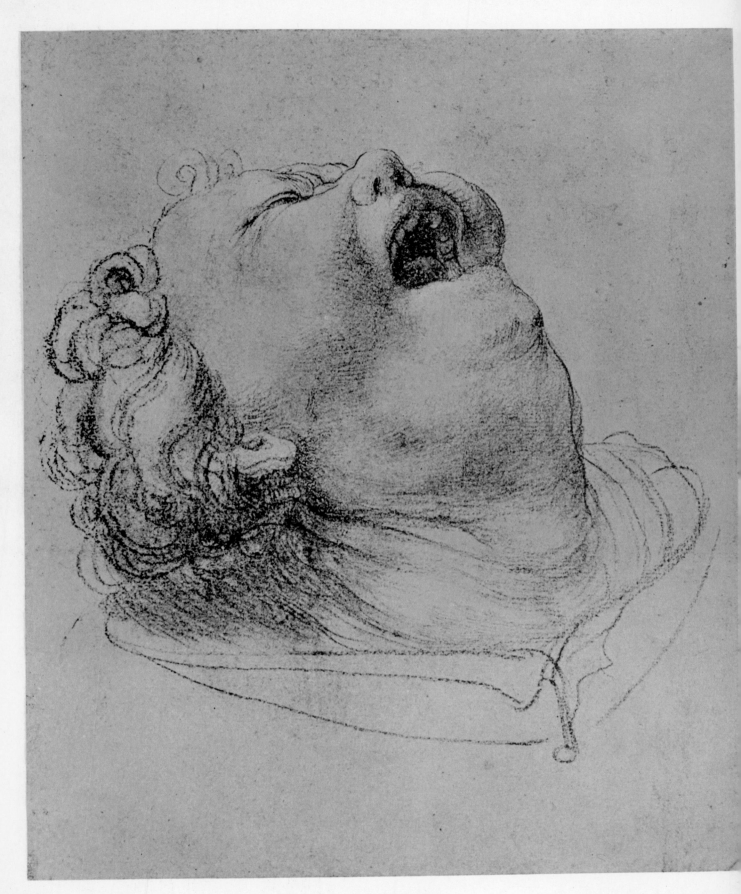

22 CRYING ANGEL

23 WEEPING ANGEL

K.l.z. 1070

24 HEAD OF A YOUNG WOMAN

25 HEAD OF A SMILING WOMAN

26 THE VIRGIN BENEATH THE CROSS

27 ST. JOHN THE EVANGELIST BENEATH THE CROSS

28 THE VIRGIN MARY OF AN ANNUNCIATION

29 THE VIRGIN, QUEEN OF HEAVEN

30 UNFINISHED STUDY FOR A SAINT

31 ST. CATHERINE

32 ST. DOROTHY AND THE CHRIST-CHILD

33 OUR LADY OF MERCY

34 PORTRAIT OF MARGARET PRELLWICZ SLEEPING

35 THE THREE HEADS: ANTITRINITY

36 PORTRAIT OF A CANON

A 1

A 2

A 3

A 4

A 5

A 6

A 7

A 8

A 9

A 10

A 11

A 12

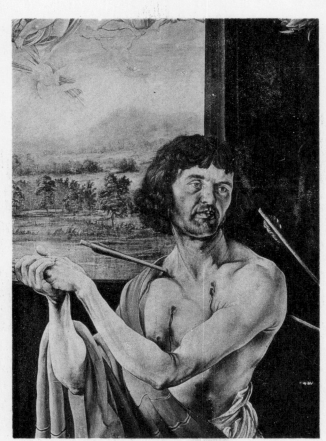

A 13

A 14

A 15

A 16

A 17

A 18

A 19

A 20

A 21

A 22

A 23

A 24

A 25

A 26

A 27

A 28

This book was printed for H. Bittner and Company, Publishers in New York City. It was completed in February Nineteen Hundred and Forty-eight. *Text:* The Anthoensen Press. *Plates:* Meriden Gravure Company. *Buckram:* Joanna-Western Mills. *Binding:* John W. Marchi. *Book Design:* Herbert Bittner.

DATE DUE

AP 21 '87			
JA 03 '93			
GAYLORD			PRINTED IN U.S.A.